PLAYING TIME

"...and the crowd goes wild for *Playing Time*!"

"Quinn Cotter is an extraordinary young man and this is an extraordinary book. Parents, coaches, and fans have been telling us this story for decades, but finally we hear it from the voice of a young man who is going through the process. Read it and learn. I did."

Dan Shaughnessy

Author

Senior Year: A Father, a Son, and High School Baseball

"I have read Quinn Cotter's book, *Playing Time*, and I must say it is a homerun with the bases loaded! It is a very well written guide for young people and their families who are interested in playing competitive sports."

Michael Sherlock, M.D.

General Pediatrics, Behavioral Pediatrics, and Adolescent Medicine

"As a former student athlete and as a father of a little league athlete, I am confident that Quinn Cotter's unique observations and insights regarding the world of youth sports will be of interest and value to both parents and young athletes."

Robert Ehrlich, Jr.

Governor of Maryland

2003-2007

PLAYING TIME

What Kids Really Think
About Kids' Sports

QUINN COTTER

Apprentice House
Baltimore, Maryland

Library of Congress Cataloging-in-Publication Data

Cotter, Quinn.
  Playing time : what kids really think about kids' sports /
Quinn Cotter.
      p. cm.
  ISBN 978-1-934074-41-1
  1. Sports for children. 2. Sports for children--Social aspects.
I. Title.

  GV709.2.C67 2009
  796.083--dc22

                                        2009006729

Printed in the United States of America

First Edition

Published by Apprentice House
The Future of Publishing…Today!

Apprentice House
Communication Department
Loyola University Maryland
4501 N. Charles Street
Baltimore, MD 21210
410.617.5265
www.ApprenticeHouse.com

For grownups who want to help kids
play better, play longer, and smile more.

To my Dad, my first and best coach,
on and off the field. I love you, Dad.

TABLE OF CONTENTS

"Kids may be inexperienced in sports and life, but we are not stupid. I've learned a lot from what I've seen and done in kids' sports."

— Quinn Cotter

FOREWORD

As I read Quinn's book, it seemed to validate many of the questions I have asked myself over the years as a baseball mom and a therapist.

1. Can sports facilitate a child's ability to navigate through adolescence?
2. Do adults know what kids think of kids' sports and do they factor that into their actions?
3. Do adults understand the impact of their own attitudes and behaviors when it comes to kids' sports?

Adolescence is a time of transition when children move towards early adulthood. During this period they are attempting to clarify their values, and find answers to questions such as:

- Who am I?
- Where am I headed?
- How do I fit into the world around me?

There are many uncertainties involved in clarifying one's identity. These questions tend to answer themselves in the mind of the adolescent as he perceives himself in relation to parents, other influential adults and peers.

Let's begin where it all begins, if relationships with parents are challenging at times it's because the teen is learning how to become more independent of his parents both emotionally and behaviorally. While tensions may seem to be about school, sports or friends, it more that these venues are the field that this dynamic plays itself out upon. This is one reason why it is important to listen to what an adolescent says kids need. Speaking from his own experience, Quinn confines himself to the topic of kids' sports, however, the astute adult will certainly extrapolate and apply his insights to other areas that may be a source of tension as well. It is empowering to parents to listen to what kids think.

Further, at this time of adolescent development, relationships with peers play an extremely important role. In fact, being involved in activities organized around having a good time, while experiencing positive peer relationships promotes psychological well-being. Teens often calculate their self-worth in direct proportion to the feedback they get from peers. Good teammates can be a very valuable source of esteem for a youngster. The reciprocal is true as well, becoming a good teammate furthers self-esteem.

Personal achievements and successes as well as struggles along the way play an enormous part in the enhancement of a teenager's self-worth and establishing a coherent sense of identity. It is the teenager's integration of these experiences, the good and the not so good, from which he learns that he can overcome obstacles and be successful. Again, youth sports afford an opportunity for this to occur.

In summary, adolescents are able to safeguard their sense of self-worth by concentrating on areas in which they excel. When they practice paying attention to the areas in which they are successful, they begin to evaluate themselves more readily with a higher self-regard. Research related to adolescent self-esteem finds that it is improved by having the approval of others, especially parents and peers. For those who participate in organized sports, the approval of coaches is also significant.

As Quinn points out in *Playing Time*, there is no question that most parents are very devoted to their children, making tremendous sacrifices, in terms of time and money. But parents who expect a return for their sacrifice invest in an economy, where there are many variables over which they don't have control.

Let's look, however, at the things parents do have control over. As children get older, competition heightens. Adding that emotion to the already complicated mix, has brought about some questionable behaviors on the parts of parents. Quinn has observed a continuum of behaviors from yelling instructions and usurping the coach's authority all the way to cursing, slapping and shoving. Things have gotten out of hand and a paradigm shift has occurred: Shouldn't the kids be the center of attention and the parents be the spectators? When such influences occur, parents become the center of attention and the kids become the spectators – to the dismay of the kids. It is always important for parents, whether acting as the coach or the fan on the bleachers, to keep some critical questions in the forefront of their mind:

- Is what I am saying or doing going to benefit the child?
- Who am I really serving by this action?
- Is it my own ego that is driving my behavior?

Very often adults believe that they are doing things for the benefit of helping the child become a better athlete, and thereby gain more "playing time", but a closer examination may reveal that their actions are more often self-serving.

Many parents, to the child's detriment, become enamored with dreams of college athletic scholarships, and revel in the flattery from other coaches and parents about their child's skills. Often parents define their relationship with their child as the athlete rather than embracing the whole child who has many facets to his personality. I have spent many years as a parent spectator, at very competitive levels of play, and have been saddened by negative impact of parenting and coaching behaviors on developing adolescents. Quinn points out that a high proportion of teen athletes stop playing sports because of the negative influence of important adults in their lives. In order for parents and coaches to promote competence, self-assurance and resiliency on the field, they must truly listen to what kids have to say off the field. Communication between adults and teenagers can be challenging. As a mother and a therapist, I couldn't agree more with Quinn's advice to parents and coaches regarding the importance of being a positive role model. Kids need adults to lead by example. Adults must have expectations that are consistent with the adolescent's needs and capabilities, which in turn will lead to more confident, flexible, and motivated athletes.

Playing Time provides adults the opportunity to eavesdrop into the thoughts and needs of kids. It is a must read for adults who are connected to youth sports. Relax, enjoy, create balance, and the playing time will take care of itself.

—Barbara Meighan, LCSW-C

HERE'S THE PITCH...

A young friend of mine asked me a couple of
years ago if I would read a book written by one of his
classmates. It was about youth sports, athletics of all
kinds. *Playing Time* was and still is the title of the book.

I was traveling to the west coast to broadcast major
league baseball for the Orioles. I jumped on the Oriole
charter flight and for the next five hours I read *Playing
Time*. I couldn't stop reading. It was real life occurrence
of what publishers put on the back covers of best sellers to
spur interest and sales: absorbing, insightful, spellbinding,
fascinating, intriguing, and thought provoking. Better
yet, it was all about youth sports—something I had been
very much a part of growing up, my vehicle to realize the
dream of becoming a major league baseball player. It
capsulated all of the dynamics between parents and kids,
coaches and kids, kids and kids, parents and coaches, and
coaches and coaches. It touched on all these topics in an
orderly, pragmatic, thoughtful, and sometimes humorous
manner. I found myself thinking that I was reading a

helpful primer for any child athlete, parent, coach, umpire, administrator, or fan. If only this book could be published!

And be available to the masses, and then all would be right in the world of youth sports. Okay, maybe I was getting a little bit giddy, but not by much.

I truly hope you will enjoy *Playing Time* as much as I did. In the game of baseball, there is a phrase, "Leave it all on the field." That is exactly what precocious Quinn Cotter has done in this book. Fifteen-year-old Quinn Cotter will teach you, provoke you, challenge you, and guide you to become a better parent, coach, teammate —even sports fan—all through the experiences and reflections of this student athlete. Did I mention that he'll make you laugh—in general, at situations you'll recognize, and maybe even at yourself. Please savor this worthwhile journey.

—*Jim Palmer*
Former Baltimore Orioles Pitcher
Major League Baseball Hall of Famer

INTRODUCTION

An awful lot of books have been written about kids and sports and some seem to be pretty good, even though they were all written by grownups. I am a fifteen-year- old student athlete. In both areas—sports and school—I am a struggling work in progress: just ask my parents, teachers, and coaches. But I have been playing competitive sports since I was five and I believe I have some things to say about the subject of kids and sports. So, last year, I decided to write a book myself.

I've played competitive youth baseball, football, basketball, golf, and skeet shooting. I've had lots of experiences, both good and bad. I have ridden the bench so the coach's klutzy kid could play and I have been a star. I have struck out with the bases loaded in the last inning and I have won a home-run derby. I have missed free throws that would have won a basketball game and pitched a two-hit shutout against one of the best teams in the country with Cal Ripken, Jr., watching in the stands. I've gotten home after practice at 9:30pm and had to face four hours of homework. I have been abandoned by jealous friends. I have been cheered for my accomplishments and cursed out and called foul names by coaches.

Kids may be inexperienced in sports and life, but we are not stupid. I've learned a lot from what I've seen and done in kids' sports. If your kid is considering whether to play sports; or already on a team and struggling; or having a great time and you just want to read everything you can on the subject—wherever and whoever you are, if you are involved in kids' sports, I'm pretty sure you will find something in this book that will interest and help you.

Without parents, there wouldn't be any kids—and there definitely wouldn't be any kids' sports. Parents are the ones who pay for the teams, choose the coaches, and get the young athletes to and from all the practices, games, and tournaments. Parents pay the bills and fill the stands: you're the biggest fans (and sometimes the biggest pains). As the parents of young athletes, I know you've got a lot to cope with, and I've put a lot in this book especially for you.

In the following chapters, through my own experiences and reflections, I will try to help kids, through their parents, pick a sport, a level of play, and the right team to play for. I'll tell you what I think you should look for—and avoid—in a coach, and how to try out for a team. I'll discuss how to get along with teammates and how parents should—and probably shouldn't—deal with their young athletes and coaches. I also write about practicing, winning and losing, injuries, school work, sportsmanship, role models, burnout, and goals. I refer to baseball a lot because that's my favorite sport and the one I've played the most. However, I believe what I've written applies to other sports, and definitely to boys and girls alike. I may not have all the answers, but I will give you and your child a place to begin to talk about the issues involved in kids' sports and address, if not solve them, together.

As you'll see, this book is written with coaches in mind, too. I have great respect and appreciation for the people who take the time to coach us kids and give us a chance to play ball and learn the games. I know that it can be a pretty thankless job and that no matter what coaches do, they're bound to make some parents and kids unhappy sometimes, maybe even a lot of the time. In order to be honest, I also need to be critical of the way certain people have done some things. But many coaches have taught me a lot and I hope they don't mind hearing some advice in return.

You're probably a little curious about the person getting ready to share all this advice with you. Mostly, I am a pretty average ninth grade kid. I love sports, hate homework, love pizza, and rarely eat salads; love movies and TV, hate making my bed and keeping my room neat. I can be extremely lazy. In other areas, I have unlimited energy. I have maintained perfect attendance since pre-school.

Like most kids, I have hurdles to get over. I guess

I'm something of a fighter. I was born with a hole in my stomach and had surgery just a few hours after I was born. In kindergarten, I was misdiagnosed with ADHD and took medicine for over a year. Up until a couple years ago, when I was scheduled to pitch an important game, I would sometimes stammer when I talked. I struggle constantly with contact lenses. My dream is to pitch for the New York Yankees. When that career winds down, I want to be a lawyer.

I'm an only child although my Golden Retriever, Holly, doesn't think so; she's convinced she's my sister. Mom, Dad, and I are a team—we sort things out together. For as long as I can remember, my Dad has called me "Champ."

Please remember, this book represents my opinion. I've tried to bring to light some issues I've encountered, how they made me feel, and the way, as a kid, I got through them. I'm sharing my experiences in the hope they will help you avoid some of the mistakes my family, my coaches, and I have made. It's up to you, the reader, to take what you need and leave the rest. I hope you find a lot that helps ease you through the rough times, and enjoy all the seasons of fun that kids' sports has to offer.

ONE
Kids' Sports:
To Play or Not To Play?

When I was five years old, on a cold Saturday morning in March, my dad and I walked onto my first baseball field for a tryout with a local team. I had my baseball glove in one hand and my dad's hand in the other and I was very scared. But by the end of the try-out, I knew I was a baseball player; they gave me a hat and a shirt to prove it.

Our family had no idea what we were doing and we had no idea what would lie ahead for us. There were laughs, tears, successes, failures, and arguments. Nine years later I'm glad to say I still get scared, but I am still a baseball player. I have a uniform to prove it.

Sooner or later, most children will get a chance to decide whether or not they are going to play organized sports. Apparently, a lot of children have decided in favor of playing, because each year 35 to 40 million kids participate in organized sports in the United States. I think that's fantastic and I wish every kid would participate in organized sports. I have been playing at least three sports each year for over nine years and I love it. In my opinion, every kid should have the opportunity to at least give kids' sports a try.

Although it might not seem all that important at first, to play or not to play youth sports is a serious decision. It should be carefully talked through and arrived at by the entire family, because (as you will see) it involves the entire family. Once a child becomes involved in sports, all family members, directly or indirectly, become involved in sports. From the beginning, the whole family will be asked to make sacrifices, whether they like it or not and whether they want to or not.

Playing sports, even for very young children, requires time, a lot of time. Suddenly, families will find they need to change their schedules and activities to accommodate practices and games. The number of games in a season varies according to the level of play. Very young recreation council baseball teams will play only ten or twelve games per season. As the kids get older—say eleven or twelve—and start playing on travel teams or metropolitan league teams, there may be as many as sixty-five to eighty-five games.

Some baseball teams also play "Fall Ball," a mostly weekend league that runs through September, October, and even November, depending on the weather. I know some teams make playing Fall Ball mandatory. I don't agree with this; I believe when a sports' season ends, it ends. When I've seen people try to keep a season going, the kids' attitudes can get pretty flat because their minds are usually on another sport. But it's up to parents to decide what works best for your child and your family.

I don't ever want to sound negative, just honest, so I must mention that some baseball teams will start their indoor practices and workouts on weekends in January. I know, it might sound a little crazy—but when you enter kids' sports, you'll see a lot of crazy things. Be prepared!

Your Time – Whose Time?

Kids' sports can dominate the family's time over four or five months of the year, even longer. Every member of the family, even the family pet, will discover there's less time to be together than there used to be. Those casual family evenings or weekends when everyone sits around relaxing and doing their own thing may become a thing of the past. Parents are usually the ones who control family time. They decide when you should eat dinner, do your homework, watch TV and go to bed. But the moment a child becomes a part of a team, a man or woman you may hardly know will begin to dictate how you spend your time. In a sense, parents surrender the use of personal, family time to the team coach. Because when there is a practice or a game, you are expected to be there.

Dinner time will change. The family may need to eat earlier or later than they used to. They may have to eat separately. The "family dinner" may consist of fast-food hamburgers, eaten in the car on the way to practice or a game.

Even your family's religious life may have to change. Lots of youth leagues hold games on Sundays, so if you might have to start attending services either very early on Sunday morning or on Saturday night; for some families, this can mean having to switch churches.

To complicate matters further, ball fields, gyms, and most sports facilities are usually not within walking distance of a kid's home. They might be several miles away. So until the kids are old enough to drive themselves to practices and games, they'll need someone to drive them, stay with them, and then bring them back home. Parents are usually the ones to do this and it takes time.

Homework is yet another extremely important matter that can become a problem, one that affects the whole family. Kids usually do their homework in the early evening; during the week, most teams start games and practices around five or six at night. Parents who were always ready to help with homework might be less available, because they're off at the ball field, pool, rink or gym with the family's young athlete. And instead of doing their homework, the athletes are with their team. They'll have to find the time to get their work done either before or after sports, whether it's late or they're tired and hungry. (I have a lot more to say on this in Chapter 9.)

Add It Up

If you look at the numbers, you'll have an idea of what I mean about kids' sports changing a family's whole way of life. Let's suppose everyone agrees Johnny is going to play baseball. If Johnny's team practices twice a week for two hours and Johnny lives about fifteen minutes from his field, then with travel time that comes to about five hours a week. If he plays two games on Saturday, he probably needs to be at the field an hour beforehand; add two- and- a- half hours for each game, a half hour or so between games; and another half hour at the end for the coach's critique: that brings the total for a Saturday to approximately seven-and-a-half hours away from home for Johnny, one or both of his parents, and maybe his brothers or sisters, too. Basically, around thirteen valuable hours that once belonged to the whole family are now devoted to Johnny and his sport. Then add the time Johnny might spend taking pitching or batting lessons or practicing on his own, plus travel time when his team plays out-of-town games. And I haven't even mentioned rain-outs or the last minute cancellations that can play havoc with any schedule the family might have tried to establish. If that's not enough, imagine what happens when more than one child in the family becomes involved in organized sports. (Parents will need to address that one; I'm not old enough to go there.)

When the Team Comes First, You Don't

Coaches will be quick to tell you to arrange your vacations to accommodate the team's schedule. Some sports extend well into the summer and post-season tournaments can limit the time to go on vacation then. Holiday weekends like Memorial Day, the Fourth of July, and Labor Day are popular days for games and tournaments; Christmas vacation and spring break are also times when kids in sports are often playing or practicing. Chances are that families will have to rethink their plans for cookouts, picnics, and longer vacations once their kids get involved in sports. The team's plans come first: once you've made a commitment to play on a team, you must always be available; they count on you to be there.

To give you an idea of how sports can really mess things up, I once played in a national baseball tournament in New York City. The tournament was played over six days with teams from all over the country; some came from as far away as Michigan, Florida, and Illinois. It was scheduled to end on Sunday afternoon. Well, come Sunday afternoon the tournament was still going strong and no one knew what was happening and there was no one around to ask. Finally, one of the organizers arrived, said the teams would need to stay over until Monday or Tuesday, then left. You should have heard the families who had flown in on restricted airline tickets. They were furious, but there was nothing they could do. Some parents had to leave to go back to work and couldn't stay to see their kids play; they had to arrange for their kids to travel home with other families. My dad was able to stay with me and we'd come by car, so it worked out okay for us. My team made it to the championship game and played and lost to a team we'd already beaten a few days

earlier. Go figure. I don't know if anyone ever made an
official complaint or not, but that just gives you an idea
of what can happen and how it can affect the family. The
people who run most tournaments are great and try to
make things work smoothly. But remember, they are in
charge, so player and family have to just go along and do
what they're told.

On the subject of tournaments, I should mention the
"down-time." It can be hard on everyone in the family.
Teams do not play all the time. There may be several hours
between games and usually the coach wants the players to
stay close by. So you don't have much chance to do other
things like play golf, fish, or go sightseeing; you need to
stay with your team. This means sitting around watching
other kids play their games, which can be fun for a while,
but not for three or four hours. We're athletes and we want
to be out there playing ourselves. Everybody gets used
to it eventually because it's part of sports. But it's still
boring and can make kids and families tired, restless,
and even grouchy.

The same applies to rain delays. You might just hang
around waiting for the rain to stop. It might stop and it
might not, but you stay there and wait just the same. I've
waited three hours for the weather to clear before we
could play. You have to be careful; you can end up making
too many trips to the concession stand for too many
snacks, because there's not much else to do. Situations
like this can mess up any family's plans. You might have
expected to be home at five but not get home until seven

or eight o'clock that night. Once again, sports took control of your time.

Hitting the Wallet

Playing kids' sports can be expensive. When a child officially becomes part of a team, the family is charged a fee for the regular season of club play. Naturally, the fee will vary depending on the sport, the community and the level of play. The higher the level and the more games the team plays, the higher the fee; so it varies, but between $400 and $800 is about what you can expect. The fee is designed to cover the costs of umpires or referees; field, court or rink use; uniforms, balls, bases, sticks, and the miscellaneous equipment the team will need to play— pretty much everything, with the exception of personal gear. Gloves, mouthpieces, skates, bats, sport shoes, and the other stuff kids like to get on their own (which I'll talk about in Chapter 8), would probably not be included; neither would private lessons (see Chapter 7).

Mostly, I think the people who run kids' sports programs and organizations try to make their sport available to all kids and their families. In my opinion, there should always be some way for all kids to be able to participate in organized sports. If money is a problem and families can't afford to pay, the team should look for corporate sponsors or find ways to raise money. Some teams do car washes and bake sales. Whatever it takes, adults should always find the financial support to field a team for the kids.

If the team is successful, then tournament costs must be taken into consideration. There are all kinds of tournaments for all kinds of sports in all kinds of places with all kinds of formats. Some teams factor these tournament costs into their overall fee; others do not. Be prepared, because there may be an additional fee for the team to attend a particular tournament. Tournaments are held all over the country, so you might need to fly or take a very long drive. Most teams will book a hotel or motel with a discounted rate, which will help keep costs down. Even so, if the tournament lasts five or six days you're still looking at a considerable amount of money. Food is another expense, along with any extra activities you might want to include. Theme parks, miniature golf, and bowling all cost something. The expenses can really add up; and if three or four family members decide to attend the tournament, the costs will increase proportionately.

I've also seen coaches become suddenly "tournament hungry" when they find their team is better than expected. As the season progresses, they go overboard and start looking to play more games than originally scheduled. This is fine if everyone is happy. But if the team adds another out-of-state tournament, the family could be facing a large unexpected expense. Try to get a pretty firm schedule from the team so your family is able to make and follow through on other plans.

For example, most summer sports camps require you to enroll months in advance. Last year, I really wanted to improve my football skills because I planned to try out for quarterback. In February or March, my parents signed me up for a quarterback camp and paid for it, in advance, as required. Sure enough, later in the summer, our baseball team announced we'd be on tournament that week. Of course I went with my team. I did not get to go to the camp and my parents lost their money.

I think it's critical for parents to try to know, in advance of committing to a team, approximately how much the season is likely to cost. It may not be possible to get an exact figure, and unforeseen expenses can arise in any situation, but you should do your research to arrive at a reasonable estimate. Don't hesitate to ask the parents of last year's team what costs they incurred. Try to avoid surprises, especially financial ones.

A Shout-Out to Siblings

The final point I want to raise is the matter of family resentments and disputes. Unfortunately, at some time during the course of any season, they will arise, but if you're prepared to deal with them in advance, they are less likely to turn into big fights. Time shortages, combined with financial concerns, combined with new demands on parents' energy, are enough to cause the other people in any family to become resentful of the kid playing sports. They may be upset or angry because they feel they're being forced to make sacrifices they don't want to make. The ball player is causing them to miss vacations or other family activities. Parents should do their best to avoid neglecting the family as a whole, as well as the individuals in it. Finding a way to make the time to do what each one wants and needs to do, and make each one's interests is important. It is very hard, but it can be done. Millions of families seem to do it.

Though they're usually overlooked, I think the ones who really deserve trophies of their own are the brothers and sisters of the kids on the field. On a beautiful day, they have to be there with their parents and just hang around for seven or eight hours, looking for something to do to break the boredom. They're away from their homes, friends and playmates. No matter how old they are, I always imagine they must have a lot of things they would rather be doing besides watching a brother or sister play. Not only that, but they can't go off on their own and there usually isn't much for them to do. The fields are designed for playing ball games and not much else. Some facilities have little playgrounds, but even climbing monkey bars can get old after awhile.

One summer, the sister of one of my teammates brought a little fake jewelry-making kit to every game. I was playing first base, so I could see her, hour after hour, all day long, stringing little plastic beads together. I don't think she ever actually made anything; she would just string those beads by the hundreds. I guess she did it to keep from going nuts from boredom. But she was more zoned in on those beads than some of my teammates were on the game.

Brothers and sisters can sometimes disrupt a game. I've seen kids who were jealous or angry about their siblings playing sports misbehave just to demonstrate their unhappiness. During one tournament, the little brother of one of my teammates got hold of a baseball. Every inning when his brother went out to pitch, the boy would throw the baseball against the back of our dugout. Over and over—bonk, bonk, bonk, bonk—until the inning was over. It was annoying and distracting everybody, especially his brother. I felt bad for their whole family. The parents didn't try very hard to stop the little guy; maybe they felt guilty making him just hang around for such a long time.

I'm always surprised these kids don't weigh 300 pounds, because every time they start getting bored and antsy, the parents drag them over to the concession stand and buy them a hot dog or an ice cream. Instead, I think parents should give it some careful thought and plan activities for these involuntary spectators. Whenever you can, try to have something for them to do and give them a chance to get a little attention of their own.

Just Do It!

I know a lot of the points I've discussed in this chapter may sound negative and difficult, but mostly, they are the small stuff. The big stuff is why you do it. I have been playing organized kids' sports for over nine years and I love it. I can't wait for each new season to get here. I love the different games with the different kids. I even love the different smells. I love baseball field grass in the spring, golf courses in the summer, and football field grass in the fall. I love to compete and to win, but even when I lose I still love the sport and the thrill of playing. During most seasons, my family and I experience a lot of the tough things I've mentioned, but we wouldn't want to miss an inning or a second of play and I couldn't imagine not being a part of organized kids' team.

There's something else I love about playing kids' sports. It gives me an opportunity to realize I have grown and changed. Don't get me wrong, I love to play video games and watch reruns on TV. Some of my favorites are *Bonanza*, *The Munsters*, *Green Acres*, and *I Love Lucy*. Watching TV and playing video games is fun and relaxing. You can't go wrong. You can't be embarrassed. You can't fail. But you can't grow and change either. Each season, in each sport, I try to learn new things. For example, in baseball, I try to add a new pitch or change my grip on a pitch I already have. Each season, my control gets more precise and my velocity increases. I may love Lucy but I love my filthy fastball, down and away, more.

There is no way I can explain the importance of belonging to a team. One summer a tragedy happened to a teammate. His dad had an aneurysm, and, in two weeks, died. The entire team, dressed in white uniforms, attended the memorial service. Together we stood, surrounding and supporting our teammate. My friend, who had grown and improved over the years as a player, had become a star of the team and was having the best summer of his life!

And now, in a moment, it was the worst summer of his life. When things settled down, in about two weeks, he rejoined the team. He belonged. We needed him and he needed us.

It doesn't have to be something that dramatic though, to realize the importance of being part of a team. Life happens, there are changes and disappointments. For some of my teammates, getting to practice or a game is a place where you focus on playing ball and can forget the other things for awhile. For a kid, it really is about playing baseball, football, golf, soccer, hockey, tennis, basketball, lacrosse. That's why I call my book, *Playing Time*.

I address role models in Chapter 14, but I want to point out that little athletes tend to identify with big athletes, and for the most part, that's a good thing. Many of my schoolmates, especially the ones who are no longer in sports, try to act "gangsta," which would be a pretty funny thing—a bunch of middle class, preppy kids acting and dressing like this—if it weren't so pathetic. Kids want to fit in with something that seems exciting and important. Sports can be a great way to be part of something bigger than you.

In the long run, the positives will far outweigh the negatives. Based on my own experience, I know when a little child scores their first goal or gets their first base hit or runs for a touchdown, all of the sacrifices, expenses, inconveniences and aggravations will fade and be forgotten.

BE THERE! DON'T MISS IT!

TWO
Finding the Right Sport, Level of Play, and Team

At one time or another, I guess I have tried most sports. I just seem to like some more than others. I go to a school where lacrosse is a very popular sport, so I gave it a try. Boy was I lousy. I couldn't do anything right and I felt like a clown. The kids who had been playing for years were great and could do all kinds of things with their lacrosse sticks. When I looked at the net on the end of the stick, I wasn't sure if I was supposed to catch the ball or chase butterflies. On the other hand, I doubt if they could hit my splitter, so it sort of evens out. I don't think lacrosse will ever be my main sport, but I tried it and had a lot of laughs and I sure gave the other kids a lot of laughs.

Which Sport? Try Them All!

I believe it is important for the child to give a lot of thought to the sport they choose to get started with. Their first experience should be as good as it can be—positive and, above all, lots of fun. There are tons of sports for kids to play. Soccer, baseball, lacrosse, hockey, basketball, football, to name a few, are all terrific, fun sports which kids can learn pretty quickly and know at least enough to get by when they first start. I also believe kids should try as many different sports as they can.

One way for kids to get a feel for different sports is to go watch some games with kids playing and see if it looks interesting. Even more important, does it look like fun and are the kids playing it having fun? With cable TV, it's easy to watch a lot of different kinds of sports, which is good, so long as you remember that the people playing on TV are usually highly skilled professionals who've been at it most of their lives. If a child picks that sport and sticks with it, they could be on TV one day too. But first, kids should take a good look at lots of sports and give them a try in the back yard on their own or with other kids. That way, they can make mistakes, look foolish and not have to worry about it.

More important than anything else, I believe, is that a kid should pick a sport they love, or at least really like a lot. I say this because when kids love a sport, even if they're lousy at it and don't really understand it, they are much more likely to practice and work hard to get better. If they don't much care about the sport, even if they're okay at first, eventually they will not do well. Then the kid will be miserable and might even make the family miserable.

The issues families face with kids in sports will vary a little from sport to sport. Some sports play fewer games than others, but they might hold more practices. Some may require less equipment, which will save some expense, and some teams may be closer to home and involve less travel time. But, for the most part, all organized kids sports involve the points discussed in Chapter 1.

As an example, I'll use baseball because it's the sport I'm most familiar with, teams are readily available in most communities and it's a very popular entry level sport for young athletes. But the advice I'm offering applies to all kids' sports for girls and boys alike.

It's All Good...But How Good?

Right at the outset, it is necessary for parents and kids to determine the most appropriate level of play. You'll notice I didn't say comfortable, I said appropriate—for good reason. In my opinion, it should be every kid's goal to keep playing and to keep improving their skills in the sport, day by day and season by season. But I believe a child should, whenever possible, play on a team where their own abilities and knowledge of the sport rank near the middle of the team's overall skill level. A team where the kids are all evenly skilled would be ideal, but I hardly ever see a team with that kind of skill balance.

Now, if a kid is a much better player than the other children on the team, he or she might slack off and go on cruise control or even get bored. It's not necessarily the kid's fault; it's just that they won't need to work or try hard to appear great. This may cause them to stay at their original skill level and not improve. On the other hand, if the child is one of the poorer players on the team, that's not good either. It's too easy then to become discouraged, embarrassed, frustrated and even ashamed. It might cause the kid to want to quit the team and the sport, forever. Kids can even lose whatever athletic or other confidence they may have had in themselves. This situation is terrible and must be avoided.

In order to establish a level of play, you need a fair appraisal of the child's skills and abilities. I suggest that a parent or other knowledgeable grownup take the kid to a field and start playing. Do a complete workout. See how they field, run, shoot, kick, catch, and hit. Don't try to find out how bad they are. Find out how good they are. In kids' sports, there's always something even the klutzy kids can do well and feel great when they're doing it—one more reason why sports for kids is so great.

Your next goal is to get a perspective on the child's ability. After your private workout, invite other kids of about the same age to join in and see how he or she compares. See how the child acts on a playing field with other kids. Do they join in and have a good time, or do they want to stop playing and just watch the other kids? Do they just want to go home? (In case a workout like this isn't practical, try asking your child's physical education instructor at school for some of this information and perspective.)

Personally, I think it's hard for a parent to be truly honest in appraising their own child's skill and interest level. Parents tend to think their kids are far better players than they really are. My father couldn't give an honest evaluation of my skills in a million years; he always believes I'm a hundred times better than I am. But that's not bad. It's much better than the other way around. As long as it is understood and does no harm, I think it's great for parents to be partial. The important thing is to try to get an impartial and fair idea of the child's level of play.

Picking the Right Team: Parents, Start Your Research

Once you have some idea of the child's skills, it's a good idea to go watch some teams practice. That way, you can begin to narrow your search for the right match for your child. You need to find what you hope will be the right team, coach and level of play. A child's first exposure to athletics must be made to be as fun and positive as possible. My parents and I wish we had done a lot more upfront investigation into some teams before I committed to play on them. It would have saved us all a lot of problems and I might have learned more and would have had more fun.

Too often, parents get caught up in having their kid play for one certain team. It might be a good team with a national reputation, one that travels around the country to play in tournaments. The mistake they make is to pick a team based on its reputation, not on whether it's the best team for their child. This is often where trouble starts. In a sense, the parents set their own trap and it can be almost impossible to get out of. The one who suffers is the kid. They might just barely make the team and since they're at the bottom of the skill ladder they won't be playing much. Then the parents, instead of admitting their mistake and finding a more appropriate team for their child, will try to work on the coach to get the kid more playing time. It can really get bad if the coach gives into the pressure and plays the kid. Since the kid is just out of his or her league, literally, not only won't they do well, they might get embarrassed and lose confidence in themselves.

Try not to be too quick to head for the team nearest

PLAYING TIME TIP
Ask Other Parents About the Team

Get as much reliable information as possible. It will help you get closer to finding the right team for you and your child. Talk to the parents of other children on the team; ask them:

- How good is the team?
- Do they win more games than they lose?
- Do all of the children get to play?
- Do the children get along with each other?
- Do the children have fun?
- Does the coach take the time to instruct the children?
- Do you feel your child improved as a player or

stayed about the same?
- Where do they practice?
- When do they practice?
- How long do the practices last?
- Where do they play their games?
- When do they play their games?
- How many games do they play?
- How long do the games usually last?
- How far do they travel to play games?
- How many children are on the squad or team?
- Does the team add tournaments as they go along?
- Approximately how much does a full season cost?

where you live, either. It might be the right team and again, it might not. For the sake of time and convenience, it will be very tempting to connect with the team closest to your home. If it's not an appropriate team or coach, your child's unhappiness will outweigh any advantages you might gain. If you find a more suitable team a little farther from home, it will be well worth the extra driving and effort. Also take the time to find a copy of the schedule from the previous season. Teams and leagues usually have websites and you might also be able to find last year's schedule and won-loss record on-line. Research like this will give you a chance to see how good the team is, and knowing the likely away game opponents will help tell you how much travel time you might be facing.

It's an unfortunate arrangement, but some teams actually hold their try-outs several months in advance.

For instance, a baseball team might have their roster for the season all set by the previous September. You'll need to check with the league to see when you should start contacting the teams you're considering. Then be honest about your child's skills and try for the best match you can find. But remember: don't be too finicky because there is no perfect team for any child.

If the child knows children who are already playing on teams, it would be great if they talked directly with those kids. It might provide another, altogether different look at the teams being considered.

One more word of advice. Avoid changing teams, especially during the season. (I did it once when my parents and I had a disagreement with the coach, and it was no fun.) Part of playing kids' sports is to keep trying and keep doing your best, no matter whether things are going great or not. Moving from one team to another is at best awkward and at worst horrible. You have to start all over again. You are new to the other kids and they are new to you. The kids and the parents already on the team might resent you. If you're a really good player they might be jealous. If you're a poor player they might not want you.

Sometimes kids might want to quit a sport altogether. This is a big decision that should involve discussions within the family, with the coach, and maybe even with other parents. Remember, quitting could send the wrong message to the child. They could start to believe that if you're not happy, you can just quit whatever you're doing.

PLAYING TIME TIP
Kids Can Do Research, Too!

Kids should be part of the decision about which team to play on. The best way to make your feelings on the matter count is to know what you're talking about. That starts with research. Questions kids might want to ask other kids about their team and coach:

- What's the best part about playing on the team?
- What's the worst part about playing on the team?
- Do they like the other kids on the team?
- Are any of the other kids annoying or jerks?
- Do they like the coach?
- Is the coach a nice guy?
- Is the coach fair?
- Does the coach play favorites?
- Is the coach patient?
- Does the coach try to teach the kids how to play?
- What does the coach do when he or she gets angry?
- How does the coach discipline the kids?

THREE
Coaches: Tough Job, Tougher Interview

I believe sports should be like school, where each year the things you learn and the teacher who teaches you prepares you for the next year. When I was in fourth grade, I had an older teacher with crazy blonde hair who used to yell very loud. My father nicknamed her "Old Yeller," after a book I'd just read. She was loud and even kind of scary back then, but I finally figured out she was pretty harmless. That same spring, I had a baseball coach who was a great guy and really knew baseball, but boy did he yell. After "Old Yeller," though, he was a piece of cake. I ended up learning a lot of baseball.

Before I say anything else I want to say some things about coaches I think you need to keep in mind. In my opinion, they are a terrific, hard working group. I might just be lucky, but I don't think so. I have played for dozens of coaches and have found them to be nice people who truly love their sports, coaching and kids. Like any group of people, some have had their peculiarities and, naturally,

I have found some to be more effective, successful coaches than others. Some have been kind, gentle and patient and some have been coarse, cold and short tempered. But for the most part, I felt they did their best to be fair and helpful to all of the kids; and I believe every one of them always had the best interests of the kids, the team, and the sport at heart.

I've seen parents try to bribe and charm coaches and I have also seen parents curse at them and threaten to punch them. Actually, I think coaching is a no-win job. At any time during the season, some parents love you and the rest are angry with you. From what I've seen, the list of parent's complaints against teams and coaches is endless. It can be anything from their child being over-coached or under-coached, to the coach playing favorites, the coach not knowing what he or she is doing, the coach cursing and screaming too much, or kids not getting enough individual instruction. Or their kid isn't getting enough playing time—always a popular complaint and a major source of conflict with parents. One thing I've noticed is pretty clear: if their kid is in the starting lineup and plays a lot, the parents like the coach; if their kid is on the bench, the parents dislike the coach. Since most kids will be on the bench at some point, there are always going to be some unhappy parents. (I have a lot more to say about this in Chapter 5.)

Coaches are volunteers, so they're sure not in it for the money. Coaching a team takes up a lot of time and it's often a thankless job, so parents, please, give them credit and respect what they do. On their own time, they have chosen to work hard with your child and the other children on the team. When a disagreement with the coach surfaces, it is important for parents to resist criticizing the coach in front of the child. I've heard parents do this and it compromises the way their child "plays" for the coach. Coaches are a key part of kids' sports and help make it all come together. You only have one child on the team. They have to deal with all the kids and all the parents. So, whenever possible, I believe you should give the coach the benefit of the doubt.

Finding the Right Coach

That being said, it's still important to do your research. When you've found a team that looks like a good fit, start by talking with parents of kids your child's age who are already on the team to get a better read on the coach. Don't be afraid to ask hard questions. If the answers are positive, just say, "Look, we both know nobody's perfect. If you had one complaint about the coach, what would it be?" You might be surprised at the answer. There's a chance it will raise an issue or characteristic about the coach that you need to be aware of. You might hear the coach has an alcohol problem or quarrels a lot with parents. Be fair, don't believe everything you hear the first time; but be thorough. Once your child becomes part of the team, it could be too late.

PLAYING TIME TIP

You Can't Do Too Much Investigating!

Questions parents should ask other parents about the coach:

- What kind of person is he or she?
- How do they coach?
- Are they screamers and cursers?
- Do they teach well?
- Do the children improve during the season?
- Do they talk with you about your child?
- Do they know the game?
- Do you feel the coach is fair?
- Do they play favorites?
- How do they discipline the players?
- Are they prompt and reliable?
- Are they honest?
- Do you feel comfortable having your child play for this coach?

It is very sad, but in a time when child abusers, molesters, kidnappers, and drug dealers who sell to kids are part of our society, it is extremely important to find out if there is anything in the coach's background to suggest anything resembling inappropriate behavior. I'd want to trust that my parents have determined that this is a safe place for me and that I don't need to give it another thought. Personally and thankfully, I have never had or seen any problems in this area. I just feel it is important to mention and to stress that parents need to be alert to this issue. Once again, do the research and the necessary legwork.

Incidentally, you might also want to ask the coach's age. I don't want to dwell on this point or suggest a hard and fast rule; but in my experience, older coaches tend to be a little more patient. They seem more willing to take the time to give actual instruction, although I'm not exactly sure why. It might be they've been coaching longer and know more about kids and how to coach; or maybe being older just makes them a little more patient. In my opinion, all athletes benefit greatly from a patient coach. A coach with the patience to explain and then demonstrate a specific technique, move or rule—sometimes over and over and over—will make an especially huge difference when young kids are trying to learn a sport and how to play it.

One coach I had liked to ask me questions about the game. It seemed like we were just chatting, but then I realized he was judging whether or not I understood a particular aspect of the game by to the answer I gave. Sometimes, he'd change the situation a bit and ask me to explain what I said to another kid, and then we both knew I understood it. On other occasions he has shown me photographs of pitchers and asked me questions. While it seemed like we were talking about the pitcher in the photograph, we both knew we were talking about me and he was offering me instruction. This was pretty informal, but it worked.

Learning builds confidence and confidence builds more confidence, at least it does with me. Being certain of what they need to do and knowing how to do that thing makes kids feel better about themselves and certainly helps them play better, which should help win more games for the team. Many times in game situations, I am glad I had a coach who was patient enough to explain something and then have me do it over and over until I could do it in my sleep. So don't think all coaches need to be cool, energetic young jocks. Older coaches might surprise you with their knowledge of the game and how it should be played. Combine know-how with the patience to pass their expertise along to kids, and you have a winning combination.

The next step is to call the coach on the telephone. Introduce yourself; say who you are and why you are calling. Tell them about your child and be honest. Don't lead someone to think you're considering coming to their team with the next Mia Hamm or Derek Jeter. Then ask about the coach's philosophy, technique, background, and experience. Ask whether they've played the game they're coaching and at what level. It might be interesting to know what they like most and least about coaching kids. Be sure to make notes before and during the call so you don't forget anything important.

Investigating and researching a coach to this extent may sound like overkill. But remember: you're entrusting your child to this person. You're surrendering a lot of authority to them and they will have a lot to say about

whether your child's sports experience is a positive
or negative one. To me, there are essentially three
components to a team: kids, parents and coaches. All
three combine to give a team its persona; and of the three,
it's usually the coaches who determine how a team acts
and plays.

Whose Team Is It Really?

Coaches come in all shapes, sizes and attitudes.
Some will be great and some not so great and some will
think you're great and some will think you're not so great.
Sooner or later, too, every kid who plays sports will end
up playing for a coach who simply doesn't like them.

Naturally, at your first conversation or meeting, the
coach will be as nice and charming as can be, so be
prepared. You might even need to wear boots. They may
not describe themselves as the perfect person or the
perfect coach, but they will have you thinking they are
close to it. They will talk like they're thinking of quitting
their job so they can spend all their time coaching your
child. It's is not that they outright lie, but I have seen
them make every single family believe their child will be
playing every second of every inning of every game, and
that by the end of the season, the colleges will be lining
up with scholarships. When they're finished, you'll expect
to see Bobby Knight, Joe Torre, and the Pope all follow
them around the field waiting for words of advice.

I was on a team where the coach believed he owned

the team and everybody connected with it. Personally, I liked him a lot and I would probably play for him again. But back then he was always very serious and didn't laugh or joke around. So, naturally, the team didn't either. Joking and laughing and having a good time is great for kids and can get you through tough times and help you during a long season. Having a coach who discouraged fun was really hard.

Another coach I played for had to be the center of attention. He was loud and cursed a lot. He's a nice guy, too, but he needed to be seen and heard. In his way, I think he felt he was the star of the team. This wasn't easy for the kids either. I guess he just missed being the athlete he was "back in the day."

Once, I played for a coach who didn't know much about baseball. He seemed to be critical of me, more so than other players. I wondered if he was uncomfortable with me because I have had a lot of baseball experience and have been fortunate to have some very knowledgeable coaches. Just wondering.

It's not uncommon for parents to become coaches. I've been on teams with seven coaches, where two or three would have been enough. But most of them weren't real coaches; they were just parents with uniforms who were allowed to sit in the dugout.

I mention these examples of how teams can sometimes be controlled too much by coaches, to help point out that the team belongs to the kids who play on it. Since sports began, kids have played, had fun, learned and in many cases became very good at sports on their own. Kids can have a great time without coaches or parents. Kids don't play alone as much anymore, but it's worth noting that they could if they had to. In many ways, it's great for kids' sports to be as big and well organized as they are; but organizing should not overlap into controlling.

Coaches have an incredible opportunity to teach. Sometimes, they miss that opportunity. Some coaches feel punishment and teaching is the same thing. I don't. For example, one time while playing first base, the batter smoked one to my right. I went to field the ball and I missed it. The ball bounced into right field and a run scored. Next thing I knew a teammate was running out to first base. The coach pulled me out of the game for making the error.

The hit was not a routine play, but one I had made before. Had I not tried for the ball, it would have gone into right field and been considered a hit. I felt that the coach was telling me and the whole world "Quinn stinks." I was embarrassed and angry. Hey, I thought, that's why they score baseball games with "Hits, Runs and Errors!" Errors happen. They are part of playing baseball. The message to me and my teammates was "it's better not to try for a difficult play, because you may fail." This is the wrong message. If you keep trying, you have the chance to make the play and improve your skills. My Dad says, "If you can get leather on it, you can catch it." That is the attitude that makes me try hard. Fear of being benched isn't.

That same team, however, had a problem executing

a routine play. Routinely, when the ball is hit into the outfield, the outfielder must hit (throw to) the cut-off man and then the cut-off man throws the ball home (or wherever the best play is.) The outfielders would continually try to throw the ball home, from the outfield. Mickey Mantle may not have been able to make that play. My young teammates had no chance of making a good throw from the outfield to home plate. Invariably, one or more runs would score.

The coach would shake his head but do nothing. I disagree. This, in my opinion, is an opportunity to teach a "rule" and standard baseball procedure – hit the cut-off man, don't throw home. It is not about a player unable to make a play. It is about respecting a routine. It is about understanding the game of baseball and knowing and doing your job on the team. Here, I think the coach *should* send a new player to replace the outfielder who tries to throw home. This would not be intended as punishment, but as a way of making the outfielder remember what he should do next time. By the way, I believe the outfielder should be given another chance the very next game. Further, he should be given as many chances as it takes for him to learn.

One more thing for coaches and teaching the sport. Coaches should explain their decisions at the soonest opportunity possible. Whenever a coach anticipates a change, he or she should tell the players affected. For example, if a coach expects to play the catcher for three innings and let another catcher play the rest of the game,

I feel both catchers are entitled to know and understand why the decision is being made. Young athletes are not just another piece of equipment, they are players, people with feelings. I don't expect the coach to drop what he or she is doing, but players should be able to count on an explanation and to be treated with respect. A phone call or even an email would work too. The best coaches I've played for were there to support and guide the kids while teaching them the sport. Without the kids, there isn't really much of a need for coaches. Without the kids there are no kids' sports.

Once everybody has done their homework and completed their research and the whole family has discussed the results, you'll decide on a team or teams for your child to try out for. At this point, there's not much else parents can do. Approach the team and coach with an open mind, be positive, hope for the best and turn things over to your child. In the long run, kids are better equipped to handle kids' sports than you are.

FOUR
Try Outs: How to Take Some of the Trial Out

I tried out for a basketball team recently and I was very nervous. As soon as I got there and started to loosen up with the other kids, I thought I'd made a mistake and had walked into an NBA tryout; the other kids all looked like pros. Suddenly it felt like one of those dreams where you're playing on soft sand. As I was going through the drills in front of the coaches and the other kids, I became convinced that somebody had put lead in my sneakers. And was I playing in a ski parka? Not only that, I couldn't get my breath and the basketball felt like a twenty pound beach ball. I even started to think the hoop was about two feet higher than it should be. I know I was imagining things that probably sound pretty silly, but when you're nervous or scared it's easy to start thinking this way. It took all I had to clear my head and concentrate on doing things as well as I knew I could.

When you're a kid, trying out for a team can be a terrifying experience. For starters, everything seems foreign and different. The try-outs might be held in a strange new neighborhood, even in a town you're not familiar with, on a field, or in a gym where you have never been before. You're away from the familiar little field or court where you usually practice or mess around with your parents and friends. Somehow the field or the gym will seem much bigger and more official than what you're used to, and the other kids will look like bigger, better, and more experienced players than you think you are.

Step 1: Get the Right Information

Try-outs can be terrifying for parents, too; but there are steps you can take to make the experience easier for yourself and your child. The first thing—and this is important— is to remember to check with the team or teams you are considering, and when and where to sign up for try-outs. Then you need to find out exactly where and when the try-outs will be held. You might get this information from other parents, but you should always check with the league or the coach to be sure. It would be pretty sad for a kid to miss out on playing a sport because you missed the sign up deadline.

I'm stressing the importance of getting accurate information for a good reason. Teams and leagues vary in their rules, regulations, and schedules. Age limits are also a concern, so know the rules. A child's date of birth will determine which age group and league they will be in. Watch out here, because leagues may use different cut off dates. Ask the coach or league officials what the age requirements actually are. Better yet—and this will be helpful for the whole season—get a written copy of the rules and regulations that apply to your chosen team and league.

At very early ages, say five or six, it's fairly simple. You just go and sign up and your child is automatically on the team. The coach will call or email you about when and where the team practices will be held. If you don't hear from the coach, call them so you don't miss out on any team get-togethers. Incidentally, don't rely on what your child tells you the coach or another kid said about a practice schedule, game or anything else for that matter. And don't rely on other people. Speak directly with the coach or the manager of your team. Even other parents aren't always reliable. I've known of parents who neglected to pass a message along to another family about a schedule change for a particular game. (I think it was so the other kid would miss the game and theirs would get a chance to play more.)

As children get older and the skill levels get higher, try-outs become a more important and complicated part of kids' sports. Teams have different approaches, which often depends on how many kids want to play. If it turns out to be more than they'll need, they may hold try-outs. If they get barely enough to field a team, they'll probably take any child who wants to play. Either way, your family needs to know what's going on in advance. Always do your homework and find out as much as you can about the team's situation as early as possible.

Knowing when try-outs are held is critical for another reason. Strange as it may seem, some kids' baseball teams have their try-outs during September, six months before the season starts. There might be some last minute changes, but usually the team they pick in September is the team they will stay with for the season. The first time this happened to me, I was really caught off guard. Fortunately, the coach called and invited me to try out for his baseball team. I had hoped to play on this team, but assumed the try-outs would be in the spring. At the time, I was busy playing football and wasn't even thinking about baseball. I had to get my baseball gear down from the attic and then get my mind ready to go and try out for a really good baseball team. I know I've said it before, but you cannot do enough research.

Step 2: Prepare for Everything

No matter what, trying out for a team is difficult at best. At worst, it can be a nightmare. If you think about it, you will see what a big thing it can be for a child. It may be the first time the little kid is putting himself or herself right on the line, to be accepted or rejected, in front of a lot of other people. Up to this point, they have probably lived in a loving, nurturing and welcoming little world. Up until this point, dreams and fantasies are a child's world. If there has been any type of rejection, their parents have probably shielded them from it. Now they must go to a strange place and try to be good at something they might not think they're very good at in the first place. And they have to do this in front of kids and adults who may all be strangers. No wonder it feels scary.

If a kid makes the team, great; but if they don't make it and get "cut" and sent home, parents need to be prepared to help. Try to soothe them and help them understand it has nothing to do with them personally, it's just that they need to practice more to get to be a better player—make it as simple as that. I love hearing stories like Michael Jordan being cut from his high school basketball team. It's most important to let the kid know what a terrific thing he or she did just by having the interest and the courage to go to the try-out and do their best. It really is a big achievement for both the family the young child, and they should know it.

I think it's a good idea to take kids out to practice as soon after a rejection as possible maybe even that same day. Any particular areas where they struggled will be fresh in your mind and in theirs. Going somewhere right away to practice gives kids a chance to clear their minds of any unpleasantness by doing something fun; they might also feel good to be doing something to become a better player. I love feeling like there is a next chapter to my athletic career. But you probably want to stop for ice cream first—that always makes kids feel better no matter what.

PLAYING TIME TIP
Increase Your Child's Chances
of Making the Team

Getting "cut" from a team is an awful experience and
sometimes can't be helped. But I believe there are
concrete things kids and families can do to prepare
for the try-out to increase their chances of making the
team. It seems the best players use these trying-out
tips with most sports. Following them will provide an
edge, at the very least in terms of being prepared.

• They try out for the team they really want to play
on.
• They are sure to be well rested, getting plenty of
sleep during the week before the try-out, because
they might be too excited or nervous to sleep the
night before the try-out.
• They talk with their parents and decide whether
they are going to stay or drop the player off and
come back when it's over. (This only applies to
older kids; parents should always stay with young
children throughout the try-out.)
• They know exactly where they are supposed to
go, how to get there, and how long it will take to
get there. They know which field the try-outs will
be held on. Many athletic complexes have several
fields. I've seen some that have as many as fourteen

and they can be far apart.

• The day before the try-out, they take some time to review what might be asked of them to do. If they can go somewhere to actually practice some techniques and sharpen their game, that's all the better. Even if they can only go over things in their mind, that's good too.

• The day before the try-out, they check all their equipment. They make sure everything fits right and is in good shape. If they need new sports shoes, for example, this gives them time to get them.

• They pack their equipment in the car the night before the try-out. That way they won't forget it.

• They pack bottles of water and some light snacks.

• They get up early to stretch and loosen up before they leave home. There might not be a lot of time for this at the tryout and they want to be ready to play as soon as they get there. It also gives them something to do to take their mind off being nervous.

• They try to eat a good sensible breakfast. They prefer eggs and a bagel instead of pancakes or donuts.

• They leave home early enough to get to the try-out at least forty five minutes before it is scheduled to start.

• If the coaches are already there, they introduce themselves. They look them dead in the eye, shake their hands, tell them they would like to play on their team, and thank them for the chance to try out.

• They try to behave themselves and don't mess around. They are polite to the coaches and to the other kids, too. Whenever they can, coaches try to avoid kids with behavior problems.

• They try to just be themselves! They don't try to act like the other kids.

• Again, they try to be themselves! They don't try to copy the way other kids play.

• They remember to take deep breaths. Good deep breaths will help get oxygen into the system, which helps muscles relax.

• They stay alert for everything. It's good to look sharp. And they don't want to get hit in the head with a ball or a bat.

• They listen carefully to everything the coaches say and watch what they're doing. They get right up in their faces so they don't miss anything. If they don't understand something they say, or something they want you to do, they ask them to explain it again. It makes them seem like a coachable kid. Coaches love coachable kids.

• They always hustle. They run everywhere they go and keep their head up.

• Even though they are nervous, they act like they are having fun and enjoying themselves.

• They are friendly and courteous with the other

kids. They talk with them when it's okay, and ask about their sports experiences or their school. It helps them to relax a little and may even make them looked less scared than they are.

• They don't try tricks to sabotage the other kids; this will only make them sabotage themselves. If the coaches see this, it could kill the chances of making the team. Besides, it might be the coach's kid. Not only that, they might get punched in the mouth.

• When they make a mistake, they don't overreact. They try to just smile and keep going.

• They do what they know they can do. They don't try to show off. They don't try to pass the ball behind their back if they are not exceptionally good at it. Even if they were, they probably wouldn't do it, because they don't want to look flashy. They want to look like a solid player. Whenever possible, they use two hands to catch the ball.

• They play as if their very favorite player is watching. They try to make them proud.

• They do the very best they can and then forget about it.

• At the end of the tryout, if there are balls to be picked up or equipment to put away, they help do it.

• At the end of the tryout, the coaches might say who made the team and who did not. Whether they make the team or not, they go to each coach, shake hands, thank them, and tell them they hope their team has a good season. It's important to leave the coaches with a good impression. You never know when they might need to add a player and they want to be the one thought of.

• No matter what, they go immediately for pizza, ice cream, or both.

I know these suggestions may seem like a lot for a child (especially a young child) to try to think about, let alone remember. But I know from experience that they can work. They won't close the gap when your skill level is too far below the team's level of play, but they're sure worth trying. For one thing, I promise not all of the other kids will do what I suggest, so if your child and another child are close in playing ability, it just might tip the coaches' decision in your favor.

Believe me, many of these tryout tips are worth remembering and using long after you finally make it onto a team. Don't just save them for try-outs, either. Start by picking a few to work on when you're practicing—right up there along with "Keep your eye on the ball!" I have also found some of them very useful at school, or other places where you want people to know you're a player and a winner.

Step 3: Build Bridges, Don't Burn Them

I was taught good things sometimes come out of bad things. If the child doesn't make the team, the coach will tell you. If they don't tell you at the tryout, they will probably call you as a courtesy. The time of the call is an excellent time to thank the coach for calling and then ask if he or she can recommend another team. After all, coaches are in a perfect position to know the child's skill level. If you ask them, they just might know of a team that would be a nice match.

In most communities, and even cities, coaches seem to make it a point to know what other teams and coaches are up to. I've had coaches I didn't know come up to me in a restaurant to say Hello. They're always interested to know how I like my school, what sports I'm playing, and with what teams I'm playing. For whatever it's worth, kids' sports is usually a small world. So it's smart to make a good impression and not to burn any bridges. Coaches change teams, leagues, and levels. You never know— you could end up playing for a coach who cut you two or three years before. My family and I have always tried our best to keep in touch and stay on friendly terms with the coaches I've played for. Actually, it's pretty easy to do, because they're all pretty nice people and like to talk about kids and sports.

Step 4: Keep Things in Perspective

In the United States, in one way or another, sports touch almost everyone; they're a key part of our American culture. And rightly or wrongly, many Americans revere their athletes at every level. We assign a high value to success in sports. Kids don't usually get a jacket or a trophy for making the honor roll at school—their parents might get a bumper sticker, but that's about it.

I think it's important for both the child and the family to see the try-out for exactly what it is— a little kid trying to make a little kid's team. Looking back, I see there were times when my family and I placed too much importance on making a particular ball club. All it really did was put more pressure on me and, in some ways, on them. It's only natural to get your hopes up, but that's no reason to get carried away. Children start to daydream about being on some great team, wearing the uniform or jacket with the cool logo. I know this happened to me. Even parents will start talking about how proud they'd be if their kid was on a certain team. It's a wonderful thing for all athletes to keep trying to improve and reach a higher level, to keep moving up to better teams. But if parents try their best to keep things in perspective when their kids are just starting out in sports, it will be easier for all of them to do later on, when the try-outs and team situations become more competitive.

Hours before the undefeated UCLA basketball team won its tenth NCAA championship, a reporter asked

Coach John Wooden if he could describe the tremendous importance of the game his team was about to play. Coach Wooden considered for a moment and said, "It's pretty hard to think it's too important. Three billion people in China don't even know were playing."

In sports, or any other area for that matter, I believe it's essential to avoid making any one of a kid's successes or failures too important to the child or the parents. Whether or not the child makes the team, the sun will still rise in the east tomorrow morning. Kids need to know that their family is proud of them and loves them.

FIVE
Riding the Bench:
It's All About Playing Time

About four or five years ago, I went to a five-night pitching clinic sponsored by one of the local high schools, a baseball powerhouse. It was fun and I learned a lot. On the second night, a man came up to my parents, said I looked very good, and that I should be playing for the best team. He mentioned one in particular. The man arranged to have two coaches from that team come to the clinic the next night to watch me throw a few pitches. Well, they liked what I threw, and presto—I was on that team—just like that. But it turned out to be a mistake. It was a good team, just not for me. I was doing what they call "playing-up." That means I was going to be playing with kids almost two years older than I was and two grades ahead of me. Sixth graders are way ahead of fourth graders, in a lot of ways. I was playing on the wrong team and at the wrong level.

I pitched occasionally and rarely played in the field. What made it more difficult was that I became the team mascot, the baby of the group. Since I didn't play much, I didn't learn much, and didn't have much fun, which made

for a long, slow season. True to our family's tradition,
though, I didn't quit: I finished the season with the team.

Looking back, it's easy to see how some research
into the problems of having a child play on an older
team might have helped us avoid being in the wrong
place at the wrong time. Which brings me to one of the
most controversial and unpleasant controversies in youth
sports—that is, kids riding the bench.

I believe if a child wants to get good at a sport and
enjoy the sport, they need to play the sport, not observe
the sport from the bench. I've been on the lower end
of the skill scale on a team, rode the bench for most
of the season, and I know what it's like; it's almost
unbearable. In my opinion, when a kid is riding the
bench for extended periods of time, something is wrong
somewhere, and it's up to the kid, the coach, and the
parents to find out what it is and fix it. Kids need to play,
designed to raise the non-profit institution's profile and
they have a right to play, no matter what team they're on.

If you are riding the bench, you are probably on the
wrong team.

Players, Not Cheerers

Parents and other adults will try to console the kid,
listing the positive things about being on the bench. I've
heard people tell kids that even though they're on the
bench, they're still supporting their team. And that if they

keep their mind on the game and watch the other kids play, they'll learn more about the sport. I've even heard people say that if kids cheer from the bench for their teammates, the kids who are playing will respect them even more. During my nine years in kids' sports, I have never seen any of this advice work. It would never work with me.

If kids are on the bench, they're not "in" the game, in any way; it's as simple as that. They might cheer and everything, but they're not really connected, and are usually just going through the motions to be polite. I think kids on the bench only act like they're happy about the other kids' successes; mostly I think it's phony. To be honest with you, whenever I rode the bench, I would secretly hope for the kid playing my position to mess up big time. I'm not proud or ashamed that I felt this way, I just did. I wanted to be in the game, playing and competing.

When I'm playing, and I see kids on the bench who aren't playing, they're usually goofing off or messing around. They sure don't look like they're studying the game—not to me anyway. Especially with little kids, their minds (and sometimes their bodies) will wander all over. You can't really blame them; it's just the way kids are. I often hear coaches yelling at them to "knock it off." The coach isn't saying to knock off cheering or studying the game. The kids are messing around. It's true, a kid might be sent in to play at any moment; but if that time comes, they just go in and play. Kids on the bench don't sit around preparing themselves in case they're asked to go into the game. If you think they do, you don't know kids as well as you think you do.

As far as being respected for cheering and supporting your teammates while you're on the bench, it sounds great, but it doesn't make a lot of sense. I believe respect among teammates is earned by how you play the game. Kids who spend most of their time on the bench often don't even feel like they're part of the team. They're just there.

I personally know some kids who are content, almost happy to ride the bench. They're thrilled to have a neat uniform, practice, go to games, and be around other kids. Some are satisfied just to be able to brag about being on a team. Unless there are valid reasons to keep them that I'm not aware of, I think these kids should be encouraged to try another team. Besides, they might be taking up a place on the team from some child who really wants to play.

Riding the bench can sometimes be a result of having too many children on a team. In baseball, for example, squads with more than thirteen players have problems getting everyone playing time. Same thing in basketball: if a team has more than fourteen children, playing time can be at a premium. Sometimes this problem is unavoidable and tough on coaches. Suppose sixteen children come out for a baseball team. It's not enough for two teams, yet it is an awful lot for one team, a dilemma. If the coaches are able to recruit additional kids, they may be able to create two teams. Unless they decide to just cut kids from the team and send them home with no team to play on, they may have to play with sixteen. It wouldn't be great, but it would be a lot better than having kids without a team. Whenever possible, it is important for the kid and the family to know in advance how many kids the coach is going to have on a team, so you don't risk getting minimal playing time right off the bat.

Getting in the Game

As I said, when a boy or girl is riding the bench, something is wrong. The important thing is to find out what's wrong. If a kid is only on the bench some of the time, that's understandable—somebody has to be on the bench, because not every kid can play all the time. But if they go for long periods on the bench, you can bet the coach has a reason. It might not be intelligent or fair, but there will be a reason. Coaches can get stuck in a particular way of thinking.

So for starters, the kid can go and ask the coach why they're not playing. The coach may or may not answer honestly, but for the time being, the kids will have to work with the answer they get. If the coach happens to tell them they're just not a good enough player, they should ask for specifics. "In what area am I not good enough?" Kids should stay as firm as they can and try to get a clear answer. After all, they have a right to know. This kind of conversation really offers an excellent opportunity for young athletes to start standing up for themselves and for what they believe to be fair. Often, though, kids need help from parents to "practice" asking these hard questions.

It wouldn't be out of line for the kid to ask the coach which areas of play they need to improve. The coach might be good enough to offer a list or say exactly what the kid needs to do to improve enough to increase their playing time. If the coach just blows them off with vague responses like, "You need more experience" or "This team we're playing is too good for you" or "You're still a little too small" or "I don't want you to get hurt," then I feel the parents need to step in and speak with the coach.

On the other hand, I once had a teammate who was a very good catcher. The next year another catcher joined the team. The coach made the new catcher the starter. It is my understanding that the old catcher went up to the coach and said, "Skip, what do I have to do to get my job back?" The coach said, "Face it, he's a better catcher than you." But the old catcher continued to play hard, the way he always did. Not much more was said, but by the middle of the season, he was the starting catcher again. The conclusion I drew from this is that a player, even if he is young, needs to stand up for himself. And sometimes, a coach will listen. If he didn't say anything to the coach, there was little or no chance that he would have won his old job back.

For parents, it's best to approach the coach in a positive way. Try not to say that you think your kid should be playing more. Instead, try an approach like: "Sara loves the game and the team and she really likes you, but she wants to play more. I'm always glad to work with her, so tell me, what can she and I do together to improve her skills as a player?" Many aspects of this situation are personal and subjective, so as you talk with the coach, try to keep an open mind, and be as fair and honest as you expect the coach to be with you. If, after you speak with the coach, you're clear about the areas your athlete needs to sharpen, and you feel you can devise the right drills or practice procedures, you can work with them at a local field or gym. However, if you feel you are not equipped, knowledgeable enough, or simply do not have the time, you may want to consider lessons with a private coach or other adult already skilled in the sport.

If you find the coach is not helpful or responsive toward you as the parent, you may have a problem deeper than the child's skills. You may need to ask the coach directly what you can do to help your child get more playing time. If, after this conversation, you are still not satisfied, you always have the right to talk with the league commissioner. This should be a last resort and should be weighed carefully. It may help or it may serve to anger the coach, and little good will come from that. It's good to remember who makes out the lineup and who determines playing time—the coaches.

Usually, coaches try hard to be honest and fair, and most really do care about the kids' best interests. The coach may explain to you that the child just hasn't developed the way the other children have and that it doesn't look like they'll be playing much, no matter how much they practice. In this case, if you feel the coach is being sincere, you might ask if they could suggest another team. I know from experience the difficulties of changing teams during the season, but I feel it may be better to endure those difficulties than to ride the bench for a season.

Coaching Tip for Coaches #1:
Write It Down

I've thought of a strategy, which, if adopted, could improve and revitalize youth sports as we know them. It could reduce, or even eliminate the vast majority of stresses, arguments, and misunderstandings between coaches, parents, and players. With much of the unpleasantness removed, kids are likely to have more fun and continue to play sports, which is everyone's goal.

Once they make the team, kids usually have no clear idea what the coach really thinks of them as players. Even the parents are often in the dark about what the coach thinks of their child's skills. A remark like their Johnny is "a nice boy" is often the extent of it. Unless there's a problem, I don't think I have ever seen a coach take five minutes to talk with a parent about their child's athletic skills or attitudes.

My suggestion is for coaches to give parents periodic, written reports—sort of like report cards during the school year—with an overall evaluation of the child's athletic abilities, accomplishments, and progress in the sport. The reports should start at the beginning of the season and be given at predetermined intervals for the season. The report could be based on the specific skills the coach has as his goals (skills or behaviors) for the players to master. I know this will mean additional work for the coaches, but in the long run, it would save them considerable unpleasantness, not to mention the time they now spend pacifying angry or confused parents.

Although I have never heard of such a report being used, I feel certain that it would be welcomed and appreciated by parents and kids too. Whatever it showed—weaknesses, strengths, attitude, or behavior issues—the child and the parents would get to talk about the report, and, if they chose, review it with the coach. If you think about this simple gesture, you can see how much grief it would save. Clearly and simply, kids, coaches, and parents would know where they stand, which is a very rare thing in kids' sports today.

SIX
Practice: What Good Is Perfection If It's No Fun?

A few summers ago, I was playing in a local baseball tournament. (To my family, local means we're able to sleep at home each night.) I wasn't scheduled to pitch until the final game, so I was playing first base on Friday night, when we won the first game. I went without a hit in three times at bat. On Saturday, we played a doubleheader, and won both games, but I was hitless in both games, either striking out, or hitting weak rollers to the pitcher or first baseman. No matter what I tried, I could not get the bat on the ball. It was awful.

On the ride home Saturday afternoon, I was really down. I had no idea what was wrong; the pitching was good, but not great. As soon as we got home, my mom made sandwiches. When we'd finished eating, my parents said they thought we needed to get to work. The three of us had been away from home since eight that morning. It had been over 90 degrees out all day; now it was after six at night, but still very hot. All of us were whipped.

Even so, we packed our gear and drove up to my old

school, where they have a nice field we use for practice. For the next two hours, my dad pitched, I hit, and my mom picked up the balls. Over and over again, pitch and hit. Altogether, we went through five buckets of baseballs holding about fifty balls each. By the time we were finished, I was hitting them hard. We headed to the little country store nearby and downed about three bottles of water apiece, along with our ice cream cones.

The next morning, my team played and won. We played for the championship later in the afternoon. In the two games combined, I had five hits.

Sometimes I wonder what's wrong with me. I love sports, I love to play well, and I want to keep improving, so that I can move up to the next level, but I hate to practice. I always have. I fight it and delay it as long as possible. When my teams practice, I usually enjoy it a lot. It's just the boring stuff, the repetition I have trouble with. I know how important it is to practice. When I really work hard at a particular technique or play, I can see myself getting better. I still don't enjoy it. To me, the phrase "You need to practice" is almost synonymous with phrases such as, "You need to start your homework," "It's time to go to bed," and "You have a dentist appointment today." Unfortunately, anything I want to do well involves practice. The sports I play on a regular basis require lots of practice. The same goes for golf, fly-fishing, and shooting. Even sports or hobbies I only think I might like to try someday require practice.

Make Practice Play for You

I think I connect practice with repetition and boredom. It probably goes back to when I was little. Like a lot of kids, I didn't know much about playing sports; I was clumsy and just sort of stumbled around. About this time, my father started mentioning that I needed to keep working. He would often use the word "practice." He would say, "Let's go to the field and practice baseball." In the beginning, I thought it was great, and we did it a lot. My father would hit bucketful after bucketful of ground balls and I would try to field them. Then we'd move on to fly balls—again, bucketful after bucketful. He would hit them very high and I would lunge after them. If I was able to get within twenty feet of where the ball landed, it counted as a catch. Whenever we had the chance, we would go to the field to practice; and, very slowly, I was getting better. I enjoyed it right up to when it finally dawned on me that we just kept doing the same thing over and over.

As soon as I knew what boredom was, I got bored. I began to get tired of the practices. We would still go to the field, but I would be out of it, just going through the motions, irritable, grumpy, and uninterested. After about a month or so, things had deteriorated to the point where, if I missed the ball, I'd throw my glove at it, cry, or lie down in the field (or all three).

Well, my father had two choices—either come up with some way to make practice tolerable for me, or find a kids' checkers team for me to play on. Fortunately, he decided to try to make practice more interesting.

He started by narrating everything—literally. He'd turn into a loudmouth play-by-play announcer, calling each situation, pretending we were making key plays in the seventh game of the World Series. It was a silly approach, and he sounded ridiculous, but it worked, it got me more involved and brought life and fun into practicing.

When I'd practice hitting, we'd sometimes pretend it was a home run derby, with him calling which ones were home runs and which ones were short. (I thought he was a little too conservative in his calls.) Another thing he did that helped—changing the name. Now, instead of calling it "practice," he would say, "Let's go up to the field for a quick workout and some ice cream." Well, to me, that sounded like a much better arrangement; and as we sat on the porch of the little country store near the field eating our ice cream I started to feel a lot better about practicing.

Finally, my dad laid a comment on me I think I will remember for the rest of my life. "Remember, he said, "When you're not practicing, somewhere some kid is. And when you meet, that kid will win." Even now, just thinking about this makes me want to head for a field or a gym and get to work.

New Sport? New Tactics

I'm lucky that my parents took the time to figure out how to get me to be more receptive to practicing. As a little kid, I liked baseball, and I wanted to be a good player, but I did not want to put in the work required to get there. When I realized I had to practice to play on my little team, I got mad. I wanted a shortcut. Nobody, especially kids, likes to keep having to repeat and repeat something they don't think they can do in the first place. You think you'll never get the hang of it and then you get to the point where you don't care if you get the hang of it or not— remember that feeling? But it's a fact of life: to improve at any sport, you need to practice. For little kids, practice might not make perfect, but they won't get anywhere without it, so the sooner they learn a way to enjoy practice, the better. Years later, when I won the home run derby in West Virginia, I sure thought about all the evenings I spent playing those pretend derbies with my dad.

As I'm getting older, our "practices" can get extremely competitive, but my dad still narrates while he tries his tricks to psyche me out. The silly games we play when I'm practicing basketball go back to when I first tried the game. One of the worst feelings a young athlete can experience is going out on the field or the court and not being sure just what to do. It can scare you till you can't even think, let alone play. I went through this with all of my sports, especially basketball. Fortunately, my dad was patient and had a plan.

I didn't really know anything about basketball—not even the rules of the game. I faked everything and just hoped no one would catch on. I would run around, jump up and down, wave my arms, and try to do what I saw the other kids doing; above all, I tried to look like I knew what was going on. In spite of being completely confused, I knew I liked basketball a lot. My dad, who figured out my whole situation just by watching me play, started taking me to a local basketball court for practice. We also started watching college basketball on TV. We especially loved—and still do—the Duke Blue Devils and Coach K. Watching them play helped me start to see how the game is supposed to be played and what players were supposed to do. As we watched, my dad would patiently explain why the ref called a particular foul on a player, what a player had done wrong, and what he should have done instead; he'd explain things like protecting the ball when you dribble, blocking out other players in order to get a rebound, and how to move around to get open to receive a teammate's pass. Improving my basketball game was a long, slow process; but with my dad's help I finally got to a point where I knew what needed to be done and what I should be doing to help. Once again, practice (and my dad's patience) paid off for me.

Smile, You're on ESPN!

When I practice golf or basketball by myself, I let my imagination go crazy. Sometimes I picture myself competing in the Masters or the British Open on the final day; or I'm in the Final Four with a minute left to play—stuff like that. No matter what sport it is, I think if a kid just uses a little imagination, there is always a way to make working out or practicing an interesting, fun, and productive time.

One more point is worth mentioning. My mother, father, and I have been practicing sports at the same fields by my old elementary school for about nine years. They have basketball courts, six full baseball fields, and everything is kept in excellent shape; it's a great place to practice. During the baseball season, we practice an average of four times a week; in basketball season, depending on weather, we might average twice a week. (As you can tell, we're there a lot.) And in nine years, during all those trips, only once have we ever seen anyone else there practicing on their own. Go figure.

Sometimes, when I'm riding in the car with my parents, I might see a kid outside all alone, throwing a ball against a wall or hitting stones with a broomstick or shooting baskets. I think to myself, "So there's that kid my father was talking about…."

SEVEN
Private Lessons:
Necessity or Luxury?

One time, my pitching coach wanted to come and watch me pitch in a game. My parents practically had to get permission for him to be there (which is another story). Anyway, while he was watching me pitch, I happened to hit a batter. During one of our lessons, he'd told me it was important not to let hitting a batter upset me; it's bound to happen, just part of the game. Well, maybe because he was there, when the next batter came up, I went right to my fastball a little inside for a strike, exactly the way he'd taught me. I knew what to do, but because he was there I actually did it—and still do to this day.

I believe every athlete, until the day he or she stops playing the game, is a work in progress, and that any additional help they can get along the way is well worth exploring. As kids get older and better at a sport, they may develop individual characteristics or techniques of their own that work well for them. But in the early years, there is a right way and wrong way to play every sport. Teaching the right way from the start will help kids avoid learning the wrong way and picking up bad habits, which can be hard to break later on in their careers.

The Case for Private Lessons

I strongly believe in getting kids private lessons to help them along as they're learning to play sports. Like teachers at school, strangers are sometimes better at teaching kids things than family members, neighbors or other people they know. For one thing, kids are more likely to be on their best behavior—or at least to act more polite and respectful—with someone they don't know very well. In turn, this might cause them to pay more attention to what the person is trying to teach them.

The ideal time to start private lessons will vary from child to child. A lot will depend on the child's skill level and enthusiasm for their sport. If parents discover that a child shows a sincere interest in a sport and loves to play it, the time might be right for some instruction beyond what their coaches provide.

Coaches are terrific, but they are mostly amateurs. They're men and women with other jobs who are volunteering their time to coach. This is great, and I believe every kid should always take the time to let their coaches know how much they appreciate what they do, and thank them for taking the time to help them to play and enjoy the sport. I know some coaches were once really good players and know how to play the game.

But if you follow sports, you know it's not always the great players who make great coaches. I believe the best coaches are people who love the sport, know the sport, and know how to teach the sport to others. And when it comes to kids, the teaching part is a real challenge.

Sports Clinics – A Great (and Cheaper) Alternative

Sports clinics can be wonderful for kids of all ages and are available for all sports. Usually they're conducted by two or more coaches and are set up to handle ten or fifteen kids, depending on the sport and the level. The coaches might demonstrate techniques and give pointers to the kids as a group before working with them one on one. Clinics are much less costly than private coaches; and the kids are with other kids, which can make it more fun. For small children just starting out, clinics are an especially good way to learn the fundamentals of their particular sport.

Finding the Right Private Coach

If it appears that a child is ready for private coaching, the child's coach might be able to recommend someone they know to be a good instructor. Or check around at your local batting cage. Another way to find a coach (and the one I think is best) is to watch other kids play. When you see a child playing well, ask the parents if the child gets private instruction, and if so, ask if they'd be willing to tell you who it is, and how to get in touch. My parents are always glad to tell anyone how to get in touch with my coach. But don't be a bit surprised if someone won't tell you about their kid's coach. Parents can be very funny when it comes to kids' sports. They might feel they want to keep a coach for themselves and not let any other kids get the advantage of the instruction. Their kid, on the other hand, would probably be glad to tell you if you asked—all I can say is—Go figure.

It's a good idea to track down two or three potential private coaches. This allows you to talk with them, compare, and make an informed selection. Keep in mind that a good private coach for one kid might not be good for another. I once played with a kid and he and his parents wanted to use the same pitching coach I use. I'm no scout, but I have eyes, and I knew this kid needed more than a pitching coach. He needed an attitude coach. To begin with, I don't think he even liked to pitch, and I don't remember ever seeing him get anybody out. Anyway, he and his family went to my coach twice, then quit. They said my coach ruined his pitching form. What pitching form? He had none.

Meet with each candidate, give the coach and the child a chance to chat, and get to know each other a little. Then talk to them to find out their approach, philosophy, and how much they charge. As far as I can tell, the costs for private lessons, and will vary a lot. But if one coach is way out of line with the others, it's important to know why. Under some circumstances, it might be helpful to get two or three kids together for a lesson. This would help keep the costs down; the kids would still be getting almost private lessons; not only that, but the kids might have fun getting their lesson together.

I don't think I can overstate the value of a good private coach. The right one will know the child and can sometimes see very subtle things no one else can spot, not even a parent or team coach. This can be really important when it comes to a child who might be doing something the wrong way, which can result in an injury or permanent damage. When I don't have my "A" stuff on the mound, for example, we try to see my pitching coach as soon as possible—not only because we want my pitching to improve, but because being in my best form causes less stress to my arm. In fact, after throwing my best games, I seem to have less stiffness the next day. My pitching coach knows the best way for me to pitch, in order to put the minimum amount of stress on my arm and my back. Any private coach who's able to save a child from facing serious problems later on is worth having on your team now. In fact, in some cases, private lessons may be a necessity, not a luxury.

The way things are today, I think there are private instructors available to teach just about every aspect of every sport at every level, and I guess most of them are fine and know what they're doing. But once again, parents can't do too much research when trying to find someone to instruct a child. Personally, I have been very fortunate. I've had the same pitching coach for over five years and it's been a terrific relationship. He has become a pal, almost like a member of our family. For one thing, he's a real good guy and a gentleman; he's pretty tall and a left handed pitcher, too, which gives us something else in common. He knows my pitching abilities, and he knows what I can and cannot do. He's always getting me to stay with my strengths and to keep things simple. When I throw a really good pitch, he smiles, shakes his head disbelievingly, and says "filthy!" He makes me feel like a real stud. I love to hear his stories about pro baseball— he pitched in the Orioles and the New York Yankees organizations. Most of all, my coach has taken the time to get to know me, as a person and as a ballplayer, and I think that helps us work together as a team.

Coaching Tips for Coaches #2: Ask the Experts—Please

Some very smart ball clubs will occasionally bring in an outside coach to help the kids with different aspects of playing the sport. If the families chip in to pay for the coach, this is a lot less costly than private one-on-one lessons. A baseball team, for example, might bring in a pitching coach to work individually with each of the pitchers. This approach is great for a lot of reasons. The kids are already assembled for practice, in a receptive state of mind, and the team coaches get a chance to hear the visiting coach's comments on each kid's strengths and weaknesses.

Unfortunately, of all of the teams I've ever played on, only one ever used an outside coach. It seems to me that most coaches do not want to give up authority, in any way. I really believe that they think they know all they need to know, which is ridiculous and unfair to the kids. At every age and level, especially in the early years, playing sports is a learning process and the kids should be given the chance to learn from experts. Outside coaches are an asset, never a liability.

The Peanut Gallery

Many adults—parents, relatives, and friends—tend to assume they know more about sports than the kids. Now, with really little kids, this is probably true; as kids get older and become more experienced at a sport, it isn't always the case. Still, at every game, whenever a kid makes a mistake or an error of any kind, at least one adult will feel obligated to tell them what they should have done differently. If a kid strikes out, I guarantee, someone will holler advice. The kid who misses a kick in soccer, or the youngster who misses a free-throw in basketball, is certain to receive unsolicited guidance from the stands. It's an automatic. What's interesting to me is that the advice people yell at kids is universal. Their tips are completely interchangeable and applicable to all sports. For example, at every game in kids' sports, someone is bound to yell, "Keep your eye on the ball!" Or "Keep your head down!" or "Keep your head up!" or "Don't move your feet!" or

"Keep your feet moving!" or "Keep your glove down!" or "Get your glove up!" "Stay back!" and "Move forward" are also popular. When I'm pitching, I especially enjoy hearing people yell, "Throw strikes!" I guess they think they need to remind me...

One of the best things about having your own private coach is that you already know the right thing to do, so you can tune out all the other well-meaning adults and even laugh a little. For this reason alone, private instruction is worth it.

EIGHT
Equipment and Uniforms: Look Smart

My father and I were looking at baseball bats, and I saw one I liked that cost $225. The salesman showed us another bat for $300. He said the $300 bats were "flying out of here." He led us to believe that every kid my age was using that bat. He kind of implied that if my dad didn't me get that bat, he wasn't a good dad. My father bought the $300 bat. I played seventy games that season and never saw another $300 bat.

Parents should never underestimate the importance of their sports equipment to kids. Aside from actually needing equipment to play sports, for little kids it's important because it's their stuff—and to them, it's just like the gear their heroes use. If a six year old has a baseball glove that has Derek Jeter's name on it, as far as they're concerned, it's exactly like the one Derek uses, and don't try to tell them it isn't.

A Trip to the Sporting Goods Store (and the ATM)

A kid's first baseball glove, bat, first real pair of football, or soccer shoes represents their first step into an exciting new world. So I think the first trip to a sporting goods store should be made into a big family event. When mom gets a new party dress or dad gets new golf clubs, it's a big deal; it should be the same for kids and their equipment. Take them to the store; don't buy stuff and give it to them back home, even as gifts. I say this for a few reasons. For one thing, helping to pick it out and being there when you buy it encourages kids to place more value on their equipment, and that means they might take better care of it. Shoes, gloves, sticks, helmets, and bats all need cleaning or oiling or both. Even very young kids should learn this and learn to help with the work involved.

Sport shoes, baseball gloves, helmets, and hats all vary in size and fit. Another reason parents should take the child along to the sporting goods store, is that it will give you the chance to make sure everything fits and works the way it's supposed to. I've seen little kids show up to play baseball wearing "lefty" gloves. Somebody figured since the kids were left-handed, they should wear the glove on the left hand: Well, it doesn't work that way. If you have any doubt about what equipment the kid might need and what sizes are right, ask the salesperson. Usually they can help steer you in the right direction.

Ever since I first started playing sports, at the

beginning of every year and every sport, my father never fails to comment—a lot—about how expensive kids' sports equipment has become since his day. Some things get to him more than others, but the cost of sports shoes always causes him to moan and groan. (To give you an idea, he still thinks Chuck Taylor Converse All-Star sneakers are the best shoes ever made.) He feels the need to wonder out loud, to anyone who will listen, how Wilt Chamberlain, Bill Russell, and Jerry West ever managed to play basketball without hundred-dollar sneakers. My dad can get really carried away over the prices of things, and, I guess, in some ways, he's right. The cost of kids' metal baseball bats always shocks people the first time they price one: easily $200, often more, and the kid might need a new one every year.

One of the great places for families with kids in sports is the used sporting goods store. I think parents and their kids should decide what equipment the kid wants and needs; go to a regular sports store to check prices; and then head to the used store. It's surprising how often they'll have just what you're looking for, and at a reduced price. A $250 baseball bat in great condition might be $40 or less. The same applies to lacrosse sticks, soccer balls, shoes, gloves and other stuff. It's definitely worth the trip before you pay full price at a fancy store. You can also bring in your old sports gear for them to buy from you.

Safety First, Fashion Later

Sports involving contact present special issues. It is critical for any headgear to be the best the team or the family can afford. Helmets should provide maximum safety and must absolutely be as close to a perfect fit as possible. When the football team is giving out helmets, parents should stand right there and make sure the fit is correct. Don't just make do with what they have on hand. If the team doesn't have a helmet that fits properly, go and buy one. If you don't know whether a helmet fits properly, go from store to store until you find somebody who does know. Your child's head is not a place to be uncertain or cheap.

And don't cut corners on mouthpieces. Each year, I go to my dentist and have a mouthpiece made from an impression of my teeth. Doing this will cost more than using the ones you get from the team, but it will be worth every penny. I've noticed in football that when a kid's mouthpiece doesn't fit right or hurts, he'll try to play without it; that's really dangerous, and if the refs don't catch him he could be badly hurt. Not only do they protect the teeth, but mouthpieces also serve to absorb some of the shock when kids are hit in the head—which in football they will be, sooner or later.

Other pieces of equipment don't have to be the best money can buy. If the pants are a little baggy, the shin guards need to be taped, or the bat is a little too long, it's not critical. But never, ever skimp on the important protection pieces of sports equipment.

Care, Maintenance, and Meaning

Since kids' sports gear is such a big investment, I suggest putting the kid's name on everything. Make labels or use indelible pens, not necessarily because another kid might steal the equipment, but in case it gets misplaced at a game or practice. Also, a lot of equipment looks the same. Otherwise, people won't know who to return it to when it's found.

Finally, I believe kids should respect the cost of their equipment, learn to care for it, and be proud of what they have. In my case, I've used the same two baseball gloves—my first base mitt and my pitching glove—for three years. Every spring, I look at new gloves in the store, but when I try them on, I realize how much I love my old gloves. I wouldn't trade them for new ones. Of course, on every team there's always some kid who has fancier, more expensive (although not necessarily better) stuff than anyone else. Kids should be taught to ignore situations like this and concentrate on playing. The baseball glove an average twelve year old kid uses today is probably much better designed and made than the one Willie Mays used. So if the kid can play, the kid can play. If the kid can't play, a $300 glove will not change that.

Be careful. The people who sell sporting equipment to parents will use what I call the "guilt pitch." They'll tell the parents that every kid in their child's age group is using a particular piece of equipment; it might be a type of shoe. By coincidence, the shoes they say "all" the kids are wearing will usually be the most expensive shoes they sell. In fact, never do all kids wear or use the same anything. Go to any field or gym, and you will see kids using all kinds of equipment at every point on the price range.

Wearing the Uniform

There's nothing like your first uniform. It might be only a hat and a tee shirt with a number on the back, but it's your uniform. I think some kids go out for a sport and join a team just for the thrill of getting a uniform. I know how they feel. There have been times when I looked at my uniform, saw the team name and my number 22, and couldn't believe it was real; I wear the number of the great Jim Palmer! Older kids might try to seem real cool and casual about their uniforms or jackets, but believe me it's an act.

Whenever possible, I think it's neat for a child to have a number they feel really good about. It might be the number of their favorite pro player, or just their lucky number, but they should try to wear a number they like. I always try to wear number 22, in all sports: it's just my number. For me, twenty-two represents the intelligence and fire to win of Palmer. Some teams also put the kid's last name on the back of the uniform. Some have really cool jackets, pullovers, or sweatshirts with the team's name, as well as the kid's name and number on them; some even have jackets and hats for the parents, or big team stickers to put on the family car.

The day they give out the uniforms is usually pretty hectic and exciting, with everybody trying different sizes to see what fits. Even though it's a busy day, it's also a good time for the coach to explain to the kids and the parents that wearing this stuff carries a tremendous responsibility. Uniforms and jackets identify the kids and the team to the public. How the kids act when they're in uniform reflects directly on the ball club. Parents might pay for the uniform, but the name on the front belongs to the team. When you're a kid stepping onto the field, you should wear the uniform with pride; you should care about it and not disgrace it with inappropriate behavior. If your team goes to a restaurant for pizza, people will notice you, not because you're famous or anything, but because it's hard not to notice a bunch of kids in uniforms eating pizza. How you act affects how people will see the team. Basically anywhere in public, even when you're out alone, or with your family at a mall or a theme park, when you're wearing a team jacket people will notice if you're acting crazy or doing something you shouldn't be doing. One other point is that you never know whether someone who could be a potential financial sponsor of the team might be watching. They could see lousy behavior and decide they don't want to be associated with that team.

The same applies to parents. If you decide to go to a bar and get drunk—and I hope you never do—please don't wear anything that identifies your kid's team.

I also think it's important for kids to take care of their uniforms. They should be kept clean and in good repair.

If the pants get ripped, replace them, or make sure they're mended. If you're playing baseball, always buy two hats at the start of the year—one for games and one for practices. When you play and practice in the same hat, your sweat will start to make it look and smell terrible (I learned this the hard way). The fact is that when players show up in sloppy, smelly, dirty, or torn uniforms, it looks like they don't care how they look or how they play. Each player on every team should show up looking sharp, ready to play ball, and proud of the team they play for. In other words— show up looking like winners.

NINE
Sports and Schoolwork: Doing It All

Sports and school work can crash head-on. A couple of seasons ago, during my first year at a new school, my baseball team scheduled a practice for 5:30 to 7:30 in the evening on a school night. The practice field we were using was only about twenty minutes from my school, but close to forty minutes from my house. My parents picked me up at school around 4:15 so we'd have time to stop for a sandwich at a place where I could change into my uniform. Then we headed for practice.

Unfortunately, instead of ending at 7:30 as scheduled, practice ran until 8:15. My family got home about 9:00; it was after 9:30 by the time I'd showered and had something to eat. Now I had to get ready to face about four hours of homework. I really wanted to do well at school and I tried to study, but around midnight I could see it wasn't going to work. So I went to bed and crashed, leaving the rest to finish in the morning. But even though I get to school early, I just couldn't pull it off.

The late practices happened several times that spring. I'm sorry to say, during that quarter my grades dropped in all subjects.

One of the toughest parts of being a student athlete, at any age or level, is having to constantly find the time to balance sports and school work. Kids may start to feel that every hour they're awake, they're either doing school work or they're involved in their sport, with no time left over to do important stuff like just goofing off.

Managing Time Before It Manages You

In the original "Dr. Doolittle" movie there is an animal called a Push-Me-Pull-You. Every kid playing organized sports will identify with this animal at some time. Youngsters get to feel as though they're being pushed in one direction and pulled in another. For anyone, especially young children, it can be a terrible feeling. There have been times when I didn't think I could handle school or sports, let alone both.

Up front, I want to say that although this is Chapter 9, I wrote it last. I felt the most uncomfortable with this chapter for two reasons. The first is that I don't want to represent myself as this incredible student who has it all figured out and can always find enough time in the day to get it all done. I don't have the time management thing figured out—at all. (Neither, I've discovered, have most of my friends.)

The second reason I felt uncomfortable has to do with this: I want to be responsible for my sports myself. It's great for parents to act as a safety net, but I think kids have a responsibility to form good habits of their own. I want my parents to stay away as much as possible. But the difficulty of balancing the demands of school and the demands of sports has forced me to ask for my parents' help from time to time. I hope that as I continue to mature, I will take the full responsibility for time management on myself. However, for now, my parents are on my team. That's good, because they have a better sense of how much time things take. They also have the authority to speak to the coach and say, "Quinn can't make practice tonight—he has a great deal of homework. See you tomorrow night."

It may seem silly for young kids to need to manage their time, but without a plan, time will become an enemy instead of an ally. Kids' sports teams often practice or play games early in the evenings on school nights, prime time as far as school work is concerned. When coaches get kids going at a practice, they want to cover as much ground as possible. Sometimes, when you're practicing under the lights, some coaches forget to stop. After a few seasons, kids and their families have a better feel for what to expect, but the situation is still challenging, and filled with both stresses and pressures. The varsity baseball coach at my school makes it a point to keep practices to two hours or less. After that, he feels the players are physically and mentally tired and less receptive to instruction. If this is true for high-school athletes, it's even more so for younger children.

Many people think kids have unlimited energy and I guess some seem to. But sooner or later, all kids will get tired, and when they do, their attitudes will change. Messing around at school or in the backyard is one thing; playing organized sports is another. Even for the youngest ballplayers, their coach and team will have a structure, and the children will have responsibilities. They'll need to be at a certain place at a certain time, have the right clothing and equipment, and also have both snacks and water packed. They'll also need to follow the rules and pay attention to the coach's instructions. All this can tire a young child.

Between the demands of sports and school work, sleep, which is important to all youngsters, becomes harder to come by. Instead of getting the proper amount of sleep, student athletes go to bed later, and get even more tired. Burning the candle at both ends can make youngsters rundown and more susceptible to colds and other illnesses. On top of this comes the challenge of making sure the tired little athlete does his or her homework, is on the ball, and is alert at school. It can be done—it's not easy, but it can be done, as long as the kids and the parents are committed to working together.

For instance, my parents and I talked about the late practices I described at the top of this chapter. We realized it was only about 45 minutes; but it's not the actual minutes, it's where you have to take them from, the early part of the evening. We've agreed that if I think there's any chance my homework or studying will require a good bit of time, I'll show it to them first. Then, together, we'll make a decision regarding practice. Had my parents known I had four hours of homework that night we could have discussed some options. We could have explained to the coach that I had too much homework that night to attend the practice. We could have told him that since I had a great deal of homework, I'd only be able to stay at the practice until 6:30 pm. Or we could have asked the coach if there was a particular skill scheduled to be taught that evening that I could learn or practice with my dad on my own time.

Again, as I get older, I'm trying to take on the responsibility of talking to the coach more and more and handling things myself. But back then, as a sixth grader, I probably needed my parents to call the coach on my behalf, in order to explain the situation.

More recently, in the middle of mid term exams, my parents and I decided that I wouldn't attend mid-week practices for that two week period. We explained this to the coach together and it worked out fine. However, judging from personal experience, he's probably unique. Many coaches will say it's okay to miss practices for exams or special school work, but deep down it seems they're very unhappy about it, because they often take it out on the kid later. Coaches might even come right out and say they're playing a particular kid over another because he was at the practice.

I believe players should try to be at every practice. I don't think it's right for a kid to skip practice to go to the movies or for some other social reason. But when it comes to school, the coach should accommodate the kids' needs. If and when parents notice the coach isn't supportive of putting school first, it might be time to have a serious conversation, where you can explain the priorities in your family. This kind of parental intervention is extremely important and just plain common sense.

School Comes First

You probably remember the TV commercial that shows student athletes at the college level. It explains how all of them will eventually turn pro—but they'll be professionals in something other than their college sport. It's a good demonstration of why school comes first. Kids probably won't earn their living from sports, so we need to learn something else, and school is usually where it all starts.

The odds against a kid playing a sport at the college level are great. Even at that level, though, the athlete will probably have to meet academic requirements in order to be eligible to play. So the younger and sooner kids learn to balance school work and athletics, the better.

PLAYING TIME TIP
You Can't Do Too Much Investigating

I really like school, but I hate homework, whether I am tired from sports or not. I get really annoyed when there's something cool I'd like to do and I have to hit the books instead. But, like practicing sports, sooner or later it has to be done. My mother and teachers have taught me some strategies to cope with sports and school work. Here's how I try to "get it done":

- FLASH IT: Make flash cards for everything: vocabulary, math and science procedures, historical dates, names, locations, etc... The effort you put into making a flash card helps you remember the information and also gives you a quick way to review it.
- NOTE IT: Learn to use a good note taking system. I recommend Cornell Notes: they're a great way to organize and record information; they help you understand the information better; and they make studying for tests easier, too. A good way to take notes on maps and diagrams is to trace them and then put them on a Cornell Note style piece of paper.
- BANK IT: Learn and memorize a small amount of information when it's assigned and bank it for later. This reduces how much you have to learn right before a quiz. Things you can bank include vocabulary, maps and legends, charts, diagrams, dates, names—most of the stuff you made flash cards for. This strategy can be compared to saving money in the bank, a little at a time, when you can, to buy a big item in the future. WRITE IT: Learn to use writing as a way of organizing

material. Put information into outline form or graphic organizers. Use memory tricks like H-O-M-E-S (for the Great Lakes: Huron, Ontario, Michigan, Erie, and Superior.) Get the five paragraph essay down using R-A-C-E-R (Reword question into statement; Answer question; Cite examples from the text to support answer; Explain how quotes support answer; Restate/summarize your position.)

• REVIEW IT: Spend five minutes a day, in addition to your homework time, reviewing material just taught. Figure out what isn't clear and ask your teacher to explain it as soon as possible. Don't let things you don't understand pile up.

• PLAN IT: Use a planner to chart and organize time for quizzes, tests, and school projects, along with games, practices, appointments, and other upcoming events. Even if parents use a planner, it is important for any young athlete to use one of his or her own, probably from age 10 and up. Take a look at calendar planners in the store together and pick one you think will work best.

Playing sports while doing well in school is hard work for kids. If a young athlete can turn these strategies into habits (it takes some help from parents), the road ahead might get a little bit smoother. It was for me.

Making Time to Play

In my home room at school recently, my advisor asked how many of us have ever done our homework in the car. Everyone who plays a sport outside of school raised his hand. I actually find that riding in the car on the way to practices or games can be valuable time. Rather than just sitting there staring out the window with an IPOD in my ear, I might try to do something related to school work. It's a great time to get reading assignments done. Reading is relaxing and helps get your mind off things if you happen to be heading to an important game. I always try to keep one of my "fun reading" books with me for car rides. Sometimes I try to grab a quick nap. I'm lucky that way and can fall right asleep.

Two more ideas: First, in the morning, I always get to school about an hour before school starts. Being on campus early gives me a chance to review stuff and get help from the teachers. It's a good way to start the day because you're more relaxed, organized and ready when the classes begin. It might also give you and your teachers a chance to get to know each other a little better. I've really gotten to enjoy morning chats with my home room teacher. (Since he's also the varsity baseball coach—and my advisor—we always have plenty to chat about.) I realize that not all children can arrange to get to school so early, but if there's any way to do it, give it a try for a few weeks.

Second, watch out for too much time spent with electronic gear. My parents and I limit my electronics time, including TV, video games, IPOD, X-Box, and movies. Electronics are fun, but they can waste time faster than anything I know of. When we took this step, I thought I had withdrawal symptoms at first, but after a little time and a few arguments, I survived.

I'm not saying kids should be on a strict time schedule every minute of every day—just that they should learn to be aware when they're wasting time, and actually taking time away from doing the things they love to do, such as playing sports. "Earn the right" is an old saying my parents sometimes use and it fits a lot of situations. For kids, getting their work done is a way for them to earn the right to play—on a team, or anywhere else for that matter. Only recently have I started to turn down things I would like to do or places I would like to go, because I just don't have the time. I'm learning to say no for myself.

I know I feel entirely different when I am able to go to a game or go to practice knowing my school work is done. My mind is on the sport instead of on what I'll need to do when I get home. It helps me play a lot better and enjoy playing even more. I've also noticed it works the other way around. At school it never fails—just when I'm looking out the window at the sports fields, thinking about a big game coming up or a certain part of my sport I'm having trouble with, the teacher will call on me. I'm convinced it's one of those rules reserved for student athletes, and it always seems to happen to me. But daydreaming about sports while I'm in class is something I definitely need to work on.

Believe me, if I can go to school and play organized sports, and be successful at both, anybody can handle it. The habits I described have helped me a lot, but I'm a work in progress in this area too. I think the main thing is to remember that school comes first—and then to figure out what works best for your family.

TEN
Emotions: Coping with Winning and Losing

If you can meet with Triumph and Disaster
And treat those two impostors just the same
    —Rudyard Kipling, *If*

*In 2005, my team, along with 33 other teams, had
entered the Beast of the East Baseball Tournament in
Wheeling, West Virginia. It started on Tuesday and finished
with the Championship game on Sunday afternoon. One
of the highlights of the tournament was the Thursday night
Home Run Derby. Each team was to select a player to
enter. To my surprise and delight, my team chose me to
represent them.*

*We played that morning and won. That afternoon,
before my mom and I left the motel to go to the field,
we cleaned and polished everything—my bat, helmet,
spikes, and even my batting gloves. We were both getting
anxious, so it gave us something relaxing to do. But when
we drove back to the stadium, I almost went into shock.
The place looked liked Yankee stadium, and the outfield*

fences looked like they were in the next town. I thought I was at a golf driving range.

And right away, I looked out of place. The derby contestants were supposed to wear their team shirts and old shorts. Since my mom and I were staying at a different motel from the rest of my team, we hadn't heard this. So I showed up in my full white uniform. To make matters worse, I'd just burned the surface of my eye with contact lens solution, so I was wearing my glasses—which also made the floodlights seem like they were right in my face.

When all the kids were assembled on the field to hear the rules and instructions, I was shocked at how big, tough, and old the other boys looked. I thought most of them could have been doing shaving or beer commercials. And from listening to them talk, it seemed as though every one had won at least one home run derby. Not only had I never won one, but I had never been in one before! I hadn't even seen one before! I'd watched the All-Star Game derby on TV, and my dad and I liked to pretend during practice that I was in a homerun contest, but that was it. The other kids asked me which derbies I'd been in and I told them, "None."

So there I was, standing in my snow white uniform, wearing steamed-up glasses and seeming like a foot shorter than the other boys; they looked at me like I was some nerd dressed-up as a baseball player for Halloween. I was getting more scared by the minute and I wondered what I was even doing there. Then they announced the order. I'd be the twenty-eighth kid to bat out of thirty-four!

Great! Now I could just sit there for two hours, waiting my turn, watching all these kids crushing the ball.

The format allowed each batter eight "outs," with every swing that wasn't a home run counting as an out. The third kid to bat hit nine home runs; he really knew what he was doing and it looked like he was going to win easily. The other kids would hit three or four and a couple hit five, but none came even close to hitting nine, so that kid was feeling and acting confident when it finally came to be my turn.

My first goal was not to look too bad. I didn't want to embarrass my team or myself. At least I could see a friendly face on the mound, because I'd been able to pick one of my coaches to throw to me. He tossed in some advice first: Relax and swing the way I always swing; don't change anything. Don't be afraid to take pitches—in fact, after swinging at a pitch—relax, take a deep breath, take the next pitch, and then be ready to hit.

Well, after six or seven pitches, I had three outs and no homeruns. It didn't even seem as if I hit anything hard. Then—whack—I hit one over the fence in center, the furthest point of the outfield. That made me feel a little better, but then I made another out—four outs and one home run. Then— bang, bang—I hit two out of the park in right-center field. I started to feel like I could hang in. Another out; then—whack, whack, whack—I hit three in a row over the center field fence, followed by two quick outs in a row. That made seven outs and only six home runs, but I didn't feel nervous: I still had one out left.

Meanwhile, after my third home run, my team had all gathered behind the center field fence with their gloves; they were screaming, cheering, and trying to catch my hits. (They actually caught quite a few; I think it was the best they fielded all year.)

I took my deep breaths and took a few pitches until I felt ready. Then, I hit four home runs in a row and made my last out. I'd hit ten home runs! I was in first place and my teammates were going nuts. I'm pretty sure my mom fainted. During the whole contest, she was standing right under the right field foul pole. When I was finished, I looked at her and I could see she was standing up, but she wasn't moving; it looked to me, and everyone else, like she was unconscious on her feet and crying at the same time.

When I walked back to the dugout, the other kids from the derby were great. They all congratulated me, even the kid I'd passed. I knew there were still six kids left to hit and I watched them, but I was in another world. A couple hit one or two. When the last kid made the final out, the place went crazy—especially my teammates. They grabbed me, and pounded on me, and kept jumping up and down. I will never forget that time. The people running the tournament had a nice ceremony on the field, and gave me a neat bat, and a trophy. I realize it was a great thing for me; but when I saw how happy my teammates, the coaches, and the other parents were, I knew the whole team had won. When we finished celebrating, we all went to a bowling alley for pizza, fun

*and just being together. It was really late, but do you think
anybody cared?*

Everyone seems to agree, winning is better than
losing. No matter what the endeavor, if there is some form
of scoring, every player wants to come out on top.

Getting Competitive, Staying Compassionate

When they first start playing organized sports, most
little kids won't remember if their team won or lost a
game. They'll remember if they had a good time or a bad
time. As those early years pass, and as the kids get older
and become better players, things change.

Each year, winning starts to be a little more important.
The games, the parents, and the coaches seem to become
more serious and everything becomes more intense.
Pressure to win isn't necessarily a bad thing, but it is
something kids and parents need to be prepared for.
Naturally, some leagues and teams are more competitive
than others, and some coaches are more intense than
others.

I've noticed that the older people get, the more
important competing and winning becomes to them. As
a kid, I think it's important for parents to realize that kids
don't always feel the way they do. A lot of kids just enjoy
playing, whether they win or not. Parents shouldn't let
themselves get more upset with a loss than the kids who
actually played the game. This can make kids feel as if
they personally let their parents down.

On the other hand, some kids do get upset when the team loses or they believe they played poorly. First, give a child some time to cry, rant, rage, or be alone. A person, at any age, should be allowed to feel sad, disappointed, or even angry. Obviously, you can't tolerate cursing or throwing things—this is where boundaries have to be set. But, it is disrespectful to ignore the child's feelings with remarks like, "be a team player," "get over it," or "shake it off." My experience has been that the child will get over it pretty quickly, if the adult allows him to. That is one of the great things about sports—a lot is happening, and you get caught up in the next play, or planning and preparing for the next game. Even if you make the last out of the last game of the season, for those kids who expect to keep playing, there is always next season. Secondly, it is unfortunate when a coach or parent puts the blame for a loss on a single player or play. It just doesn't work that way; games are not won or lost on a single event.

I do think adults can help in two ways. The first is, after the game, when things have calmed down, ask the child, help the child figure out what skill could be improved, and then give the child opportunity to get out and work on that skill as soon as possible. Also, my Dad always tells me, "You may not see the improvement right away, but you will, soon, I promise you that." That's enough to keep me practicing. The second thing adults can do, again, after things have calmed down, is to emphasize the positive aspects of the child's game, or good things about the team. A lot depends on how adults position winning and losing.

Awhile ago, I really wanted a pair of white golf shoes. Around the same time, I'd been pitching poorly, but I was scheduled to start a game at a tournament at Penn State. On the way to the game, my mom was driving and I was nervous. Mom leaned over to me and said, "Quinn, if you pitch well today, I'm going to buy you a new pair of white golf shoes." I asked what would happen if I didn't pitch well. Mom said, "I'm going to buy you a new pair of white golf shoes." We smiled at each other. It sort of put the whole thing into perspective. Guess what? I got a new pair of white golf shoes.

I was taught to see the beauty of sports. Whenever we go to our field to practice, my father will always tell us to take a minute to look around at the whole scene. The smells, the green grass, the blue sky, the infield dirt, and the white lines, to him, and now to me, make a really beautiful scene. The same applies to football fields and stadiums; even basketball courts can be pretty if you look at the wood and the way the colorful lines are painted. My dad also taught me there is no such thing as an ugly golf course or trout stream. Some may be prettier than others, but in their own way, they are all beautiful to look at.

For some kids, me included, though winning is the goal, there's a lot more to enjoy about just playing the game. The kids are fun to play with and to watch. At every game, something very funny always seems to happen to give everybody a big laugh. Then some klutzy kid will make a major-league play and knock everyone's socks off. Whether you win or lose, when the game is over, there's always a lot to be thankful for and to appreciate. First, just that the kids are healthy enough to go onto a field or a court and play a game is a wonderful thing; if no one gets injured, that's another reason to be grateful. And if the kids tried their best, nobody should ever criticize them. Sometimes, I see how parents react when their kid's team loses, and I wonder to myself if they ever played ball at all themselves. They just don't seem to get it. When I watch the Yankees lose the World Series, I can see the players are sad, but they get over it. By the time they make the major leagues, the guys have probably played enough games to know you're going to lose some of them.

Two days after I won the home run contest, our team was playing in the semi-final game. If we won, we'd play for the championship. The game was close and the teams were evenly matched. They would score and we would score. In the bottom of the last inning, we were behind by two runs and had men on first and second with two outs. It was my turn to bat. Everyone knew I was the kid who'd just won the home run derby. The other team and their fans were probably expecting me to hit a home run and win the game. To tell you the truth, I was too. I wasn't over confident; I just knew I could hit another home run. After all, it was the same ball park. Well, I got the pitch I wanted and I hit it deep out to center field, just like I'd hit them in the derby, only I hit this one about eight feet shorter. The outfielder stood there, caught it, and the game was over. We'd lost and left for home.

Kids' sports can be an emotional roller-coaster ride for kids and adults. The whole family will discover that the movie was wrong; there is crying in baseball, lots of crying. I've had games when I played poorly and cried. There is also crying in every other sport kids may play and not only by the children who are playing. My mom still gets a little misty whenever she looks at the pictures they took when I won that derby. If they get to watch their grandchildren play, you can bet, at some point, that the grandparents will probably cry. Some brothers and sisters will also cry, even if for different reasons, as I already discussed.

Kids might cry when they play lousy or when they play great. I've seen kids and parents cry at a baseball game for no reason at all that I could see. But as a guy once said, "That's baseball," and I believe "That's kids sports."

When I was eight years old, I had the honor of playing against a child who had cerebral palsy. He was a really neat kid and always had a big smile on his face. His illness made it very difficult for him to walk, but whatever he did and wherever he went, he tried his best and kept smiling. You could just tell he really loved being there at the game. He seemed proud of his team and his uniform. Sometimes you can sense when a kid really loves being involved in kids' sports.

I don't remember much about the actual game, but I remember when he came up to bat, I was cheering for him and so was everyone else. He could barely hold the bat, and it was really tough for him to try to swing at the ball. But, sure enough, he got a hit. Not just a little dribbler, but a real hit. When it happened, everybody stood and cheered. Watching him trying to get down the base line to first was enough to make you admire his guts and drive. When he was safe at first base, the whole place went crazy. Many people cried; I know my parents both got teary. As I looked at the whole scene, with this kid standing there on first base, grinning from ear to ear, I thought to myself, this game really is great. I will never forget that boy. Everyone at that little field knew he was the star and the hero.

Making Strides, Losing Friends: Coping with Jealousy

Sometimes in kids' sports, you feel like you're on top of the world. Other times, you just want to be by yourself and sulk, brood, cry, or all three. There might also be times when people do things to hurt your feelings and you don't even know why.

For me, it all started in the third grade. Along with some of my classmates and teammates on a local recreation council team, I tried out for what they call a travel team. A higher and more competitive level of play than the recreation league, the travel team also had two levels—an A team and a B team. I was the only one on our team to make the A team. Immediately, my classmates started treating me differently. They were less friendly, a little frosty, left me out of games at school, and even started ignoring me at recess and lunchtime.

In the fourth grade, I went to a pitching camp. One night, a couple of coaches watched me, liked the way I threw. and invited me to join a team in what is considered the highest level for baseball competition in the whole Baltimore area: the Metro league. I was thrilled and excited to be playing on this team. Twice each week, I'd change into my uniform in the boy's room right after school; then my parents would pick me up, and we'd drive to the games. I was having fun, but something was wrong. Though the girls in my class were always really nice, the boys all seemed to be getting together to freeze me out. The temperature dropped even lower when I'd call some of them to get together for a play date and they wouldn't even call me back. Once I got the message, I just stopped calling.

In fifth grade, I was invited to try out for one of two openings on a team, ranked as one of the top five kid's baseball teams in the country. I made the team. Around the same time, while going for a rebound during a basketball game at recess, I accidentally bumped into a kid. I didn't hurt him, I just bumped him and he fell down. The kids all told the teachers I hit the kid on purpose, which was just not true. That same evening our school sponsored a fundraiser at Pizza Hut. The kid I'd bumped into was sitting at a table with all the other kids and their parents. My dad encouraged me to go over and say "Hi" and ask how he was doing. I walked over alone and did it. No one, including the parents at the table, said anything to me, or even looked at me. I understood then, for the first time, that it was the parents who had been controlling the thermostat. And that's how it stayed until we all graduated from elementary school in June. I had known these kids for five years, and I actually thought they were my pals. I loved the school and it was my last year there, and I'd expected it to be a terrific one. It was kind of sad. Fortunately, my teacher was a real pal, and he made things a lot better.

Eventually I learned from people who knew the situation and the children, that these kids were jealous. I was pretty young and didn't really understand how jealousy can work and what it can do to people. Those kids all had the same opportunities I had. We were all at the same school with the same practice field I used with my parents. They all seemed to have fathers who were former athletes—or at least said they were—so they could have gone to the field every evening the way we did. Just because I was willing to keep working to become a better ballplayer, they decided to turn against me.

We know a family whose children are all terrific swimmers. They seem to swim the way I play ball, all the time. I've called them during a snow storm to see if they want to go sledding, and their mother will tell me they've gone to swimming practice. One of the kids has a chance at the Olympic swimming team and I'm thrilled for him. I hope he wins every Olympic event he enters. He and his family have worked hard for years and years; they earn every trophy and medal they get. I sure hope their friends all know how hard they work and don't get jealous of them or treat them lousy. They're a great family and I wouldn't want them to feel hurt.

In a way, I felt sorry for the boys back in elementary

school. I still don't see how they could have enjoyed hurting me. In spite of the unpleasantness of the year, a lot of really neat things happened for me and each one just seemed to make them more and more miserable. In my opinion, if someone is a real friend, they're glad for any good things you do or any nice breaks you get. Unfortunately, when some people see a friend improve at their sport and move up level by level, they just won't be happy for the kid. They're the people who might get bitten by the "green monster," and I don't mean the one at Fenway Park.

ELEVEN
Sportsmanship: Put It in Your Vocabulary, Please

Most tournaments are played at sports complexes with anywhere from six to twelve fields, so several games can take place at the same time. This particular, highly competitive national baseball tournament, though it was sanctioned by a major sports association, was held at a little place with only two fields in a lousy area right in the center of a large city. There was only one grandstand, so all the parents from all of the teams had to sit bunched together. It was also extremely hot, so you can just imagine how loud and nasty it got when the games were going on.

We'd won all four of our first four games; so had the hometown team. We were scheduled to play them next. That day, our team arrived at the field about ninety minutes before game time, as usual, to loosen up, stretch and get ready to play. When we walked inside the complex, we were amazed to see the place already overflowing with the other team's fans. Our parents couldn't even find a place to sit; the noise was deafening; the game was still over an hour away. The parents of some of our players had heard this team had an interesting strategy. Their plan was to intimidate everybody—big time! Not only would their team, their coaches, and their fans try to intimidate and frighten our team; they'd try to make sure the umpires were scared as well. From what I was hearing and seeing (not an umpire in sight), it looked to me like their strategy was going to work.

By game time the place was going crazy. The stands were packed with the other team's screaming fans; I don't mean they were cheering; they were screaming like lunatics. The umpires stayed hidden somewhere until a few seconds before the game was supposed to begin, then they walked out and started it immediately! I wasn't scheduled to pitch, so I was playing first base, which put me almost directly in front of the other team's dugout. It was one time I wished I was an outfielder. From the moment we took the field to start our infield warm-ups, the other team and their coaches were hollering and calling me every foul name they could think of and believe me, they thought of a lot.

I must admit, I was a little rattled, but not as much as I'd thought I would be. The home team was big, loud, and aggressive, but they were better at cursing than baseball. After awhile I just tuned them out and played my game. And when they realized we were better than they were, they amped up the cursing and screaming to try and make up for their lack of skill. All game long, their fans kept screaming, their team and coaches kept hollering and cursing, but my team kept playing well. We beat them by

*five or six runs and enjoyed doing it. But we made sure
not to act like we did. Those fans would have started a
fight over anything. We didn't want to do anything to get
them stirred up any more than they already were. When it
was finally over, I'm not sure who left the field the fastest,
my team or the umpires, who looked like dark blue streaks
going out the gate.*

*Before that happened, we were supposed to line up,
high five, and say the traditional "Nice game." We did
it, but it was one of the phoniest scenes I've ever seen.
Except for winning, there was nothing nice about the
game at all.*

My parents like to say good things sometimes come
from bad things, and in the case of this tournament,
they're right. Playing under those ugly conditions
taught me something I will remember for a long time.
When teams or players go out of their way to act in an
unsportsmanlike manner, I believe, it can mean they're
either nervous and unsure of themselves, or trying to cover
up for a lack of talent or skill. They may not believe they're
able to win without using underhanded tactics or illegal
methods. Without having actually played under those
conditions, it might have been a long time before I learned
this lesson.

Sportsmanship in Action—and Absence

The dictionary defines a sportsman as someone who
participates in athletic or sporting activities, and who

behaves with courtesy, generosity, and fairness toward opponents and their sport—win or lose. Sportsmanship is when a person behaves with these things in mind. It seems so simple that you would think, especially around kids, sportsmanship would be an automatic behavior; and most of the time it is.

I believe the majority of coaches, parents, and fans in kids' sports, preach, teach, and practice sportsmanship to the best of their ability. There are exceptions, but overall, from what I have seen, most coaches and parents consider sportsmanship an important part of playing sports—something they attempt to follow personally and to teach the children. I have seen sportsmanship close up and I know what it looks like. It is when the son of a major league player (a kid I've just beaten) comes up to me to tell me I pitched a great game. It is when the opposing teams line up along the baselines and say a prayer for a coach who's in the hospital suffering from a stroke. It is when kids I played with long ago are still pals.

Former UCLA basketball coach John Wooden said, "Sports doesn't build character, it reveals it." When someone shows up at the field or the gym, they pretty much arrive as the person they really are, the person they've been taught to be at home. If this person—whether adult or a kid—is a genuine jerk, they might be able to hide it for a while but their true personality will be revealed pretty quickly. Tempers might be lost, nerves frayed, patience tried. Sooner or later, the real person will show through. When that time comes, there's no place for them to hide, and everybody will know it.

In the beginning of a season, at practices and try-outs, for example, all the parents and the coaches act very nice. They're respectful, patient, and polite to everyone. Some stay that way. Others, as the season goes along, will be unable to control themselves. In my experience, courtesy is directly connected to emotions. When they're in a great mood, people are more likely to act courteously toward others. When they're upset, for any reason, courtesy sometimes disappears. For instance, the first time some official makes what they consider a bad call, they might get angry and start ragging on the official.

Like with the unsportsmanlike team, though, I've noticed that the loudest, crudest, most disruptive parents are often those who have the least confidence in their children's ability to perform or to play well. The kid might be a really good player, but if the parent has some doubts, they will go way overboard to try and make sure their kid's team wins. (Every now and then, for fun, I'll test my theory and I find it's usually right on target.)

I've also noticed that when coaches lose their control they rarely get it back. Once a coach starts to curse, yell, or become impatient with the kids, they will usually stay this way for the whole season. I guess they figure once everybody knows they're hotheads, what's the difference? Just like the pickle, it usually doesn't go back to being a cucumber. Anger, including bad language and short tempers, is a problem with a lot of coaches. From what I've observed, when coaches get really angry, for whatever reason, they lose their ability to coach effectively and things start to fall apart. When they get angry at the kids and the team, everybody suffers.

I once played for a coach who would get angry a lot, especially when we lost. Whether we got really stomped or just lost a close game, he'd be furious at us. After the game he'd curse us out big time, sometimes as a team, and other times as individuals and sometimes both. He cursed more at me in one day than I've heard my parents curse in my entire life. He rarely discussed the mistakes we made or said anything constructive; he just gave us a plain old tongue lashing. Frankly, he showed us very discourteous behavior. Then he would make us run. This approach didn't help us to understand what we were doing wrong. So from not being coached or taught how to improve, our team stayed the same. We kept making the same mistakes game after game, and the coach got angrier and angrier. None of us liked it, but gradually we just got to expect him to be that way and learned to tune him out. It was a shame, because other than the cursing, that coach is a nice guy who loves the sport.

Now, the first time he blew up at us, if some of the parents had approached him and explained that his behavior wasn't acceptable, that he wasn't helping the kids improve their play, and that cursing wouldn't correct their mistakes, everything might have been different. I realize young ballplayers can be frustrating, but coaches should know up front that things which can really get coaches ticked-off are going to happen a lot. I believe angry coaches should take a cooling-off period. Then, for the next practice, prepare a list of what the team did wrong. Show them how they should have played and what they should have done and let the kids practice the right way to do things. My mom says coaches should approach things like teachers do. With kids, it's best to teach when you've got what she calls an "educable moment." When kids have just lost a game, it's usually not a good time to start teaching; it's definitely the wrong time to yell abuse.

There's also such a thing as quiet abuse. You can see this in the "cold shoulder" approach to discipline. A lot of coaches will ignore a kid when they feel the kid needs discipline for poor play. They seem to believe that if kids feel left out they'll play better. I have never, ever seen this work. I think the coach's cold shoulder only causes the kid to feel he or she is not part of the team, to lose confidence, and, if anything, to play worse.

When a kid needs discipline, for whatever reason, coaches should consider just sitting down and talking to them about what they did or didn't do. They should make it a point to tell the kid that they are part of the team and that they have a responsibility to behave and play the best they can. If it is a serious problem, the coach should bring the parents into the conversation. That way, everyone knows what's going on and there's a better chance that together they'll solve the problem and improve the situation.

A Rule of Sportsmanship: Stand Up to Bullies

When coaches or other adults carry criticism too

far and get too rough on the kids, it can be harmful. Not every kid takes criticism the same way. Some kids are cooler than others, and let the hollering and cursing roll off their backs. Other kids may really take it to heart and start to feel inferior, or even think that they're bad people. In kids' sports, everything should be done to make the kids the main concern. So, my suggestion is to speak up in the beginning. The first time a parent or a coach goes over the top with their behavior, they need to be told to control themselves. Because eventually, their behavior will be harmful to the kids and the team.

The same applies to the kids. The first time a kid goes berserk with anger, cursing, or tantrums, the coach should step up and talk with them. Like adults, if kids can get away with inappropriate behavior just once, they'll probably do it again and again. I have played with lots of kids who were allowed to act like jerks. One kid I played with was always annoying me. Everybody knew it, but nobody ever said anything—maybe because his father was one of the coaches. Finally I had to confront this kid in the dugout, right in front of the whole team. Being a typical bully, he backed down, walked away, and never bothered me again. Immediately, all of my teammates told me how glad they were that I'd done it; he'd been bugging everybody on the team all year.

I think it would be good for every team to have a group of three or four parents serving as a behavior committee. Then, if anyone's behavior became discourteous, they could step in on behalf of all the parents. This would solve the problem of parents being afraid to confront the coach (or each other) on their own. What's more, judging from the crazy things I hear of parents doing these days, it might stop some small problems before they get to be big problems, you just never know. I have never seen a committee like this, but I've wished my teams had one, plenty of times.

Try a Little Praise

In my opinion, if everyone involved in kids' sports were a little more generous, it would probably get more kids involved in sports and keep them playing for a longer time. I think everyone should start by being more generous with compliments. I don't mean go overboard praising every play, just honest sincere compliments. Everybody appreciates one of these, especially little ball players. When kids are learning their game, they often feel unsure of themselves and what they're doing; when someone congratulates them on something they did, they love it. And while most kids get used to hearing their parents praise what they do, if another adult says something nice it makes their day. When I make a nice play at first base and the other team's coach says, "Nice pick, twenty-two," I feel really good. Having another kid compliment my play is a great feeling, too. When I'm pitching and one of my teammates makes a nice play, I always try to say something to let them know I appreciate what they did. I'm sincere, too, because if the fielders don't do their jobs, I won't be on the mound very long.

Some coaches are good at compliments. Others apparently don't believe in paying too many. They might be afraid to give the kid a big head; they might not want to risk the kid playing less hard. Either way, I think they're missing the point. In every sport at every level, during every game, every player will make a mistake and every player will do something good. If coaches are going to holler about the mistakes, they should also remember to praise what went right. Even better, be specific in your praise. For a kid, and the team, there's a big difference between hearing "Good job, buddy," and "I like the way you tracked that ball!" One is nice but not very memorable. The other shows that you are really watching how the kid plays, and judging how well the kid is learning the game; what's more, the other kids hear this and they'll be thinking about tracking the ball on their next turn in the field. In fact, a good coach uses praise to coach and teach the game.

Don't wait for a kid to kick the winning goal, sink the winning basket, or pitch a shut-out. To a kid, one single compliment might make the difference in whether or not they like playing sports. It might also give the kid more confidence and self-respect. When this happens, the kid will probably play better and help the team play better, which is what any coach is after in the first place. I think everyone, not just coaches, should be more generous with their praise of young athletes. If any adult ever wants to see a kid perk up, just tell them they look great in their uniform. (It might even make the adult feel good, too.)

When a kid gets a compliment, it's appreciated, maybe more than anyone ever knows. And it just might be the only compliment that kid has received in a long, long time.

A Lesson in Fairness

When a team loses, there are usually a lot of plays which cause the loss. Coaches should never pick out one mistake by any player to blame the loss on. I have seen this done and I know it makes the kid feel awful. Interestingly, I've never heard a coach say, "Sorry guys, we were just out-coached today."

Nevertheless, good teams win and lose games as a team. I believe the opposite is also true. If a kid scores the winning goal or gets the winning hit at the end of the game, that's great; but it was the efforts of the whole team that put them in a position to win at the end. Someone must have been the first person to say, "Life isn't fair." If whoever it was meant "life" to include sports, you can bet he was no athlete or he wouldn't have said anything so negative and stupid. I'm not old enough to know all about life and fairness, but I've played enough sports to know that sports are fair. Sports were originally invented to be fair. The basic rules of every game are written to be fair to all sides. In fact, the rules are there to eliminate unfairness. Things happen in sports that may seem unfair, but they usually happen because the people in charge decided to do things their way instead of the way, the sport was meant to be played.

I doubt if Abner Doubleday ever expected pitchers to intentionally hit batters or players to inject themselves with chemicals that might make them play better. And I don't think Dr. James Naismith ever imagined players taking money to score fewer points in a game or some fan throwing a battery that would hit the mother of the other team's best player. Whether it's the coach who plays his own kid while a better player rides the bench, or parents who yell and boo enough to make a little kid leave the field in tears, it isn't the sport being unfair, it's the people who try to mess with the game. If you've ever played sports, even for a little while, you've seen things generally even out. By the end of the season, the good teams will have won more games than the poorer teams and the good players will have played better than the weaker ones. Those calls the officials made that seemed to go against your team will be balanced by calls made in your team's favor. In my opinion, when sports are played as they were meant to be played, without people changing or ignoring the rules, they are among the fairest things we have in life, and I think kids should have the opportunity to enjoy them that way.

TWELVE
Injuries: When Band-Aids Aren't Enough

Last summer was an exciting time. My team had decided to play in a six-day baseball tournament in Myrtle Beach, South Carolina. I was really thrilled. Not only was it supposed to be a good tournament, but we were going to stay a nice hotel, and I was going to bring my golf clubs and get to play a few fancy courses. We flew in early, and our first game wasn't until later that night, so I was able to get in a round of golf. The weather was beautiful and it looked like we were going to have a great week.

When we arrived that evening for the game, the field was already lit up. It was a gorgeous complex and the fields were in great shape. I was playing first base. In the first inning, the other team had a runner on third base with one out. The next batter hit a hard ground ball to our third baseman. He fielded the ball, held the runner, and threw across to me. I could see the kid on third break for home. Just as the batter got there I touched first base, felt a bump on my leg, and threw the ball home to keep the kid from scoring.

After the play my leg hurt a little, but I didn't see any blood so I kept on playing and didn't say anything to anyone. But as I was getting ready to bat in the fourth inning, I looked down and saw my sock was cut; I could also see my leg and it had a hole in it. I batted anyway. When our inning was over, I went to one of our coaches and asked him if he had a band-aid. He looked at my leg and said the band-aids he had were too small—I'd need to go to our head coach, he had the big band-aids. It struck me as kind of funny that you had to work your way up to head coach before you could carry the big band-aids (one of the many perks of being a head coach, I guess).

Our head coach took one look at my leg and said I needed to go right to a hospital emergency room, which was exactly correct. I found my mom, we got in the car, and away we drove—only we didn't know where we were going. We asked people for directions but kept getting lost. Finally, my mom called 911 and explained what was happening; they were very nice and stayed on the phone long enough to guide us to the hospital. By then it was pretty late and the ER was very busy. We had to wait for about two hours before the doctor was ready to work on me. He turned out to be really nice; to keep my mind off the needlework he was performing, he talked a lot about the Yankees. That made me think to myself, How would Derek Jeter handle this? I remembered seeing him writhing in pain when he dislocated his shoulder. It helped me to realize my wound wasn't as bad as what he'd gone through.

Back at the hotel, as I was dozing off, I thought about what happened to me. At the time, everything was moving so fast, and I was so focused on the kid trying to score from third base, and on making a good throw to our catcher, that all of it was a little hazy. I thought about a lot of things, like how one simple play could affect the whole trip—baseball, golf, fishing and all the things I wanted to do. Then I thought about the kid who spiked me. I guess I'll never know for sure, but I'll probably always wonder if he did it on purpose to break up the play. I know stuff like that goes on in sports at the higher levels, but I'd never seen it happen in kids' sports, then or since. Which doesn't mean it doesn't happen, just that I have never seen anyone injure anyone on purpose. I forced myself to fall asleep believing it was an accident. I knew I'd sleep better that way.

Well, needless to say, all our plans changed—no more golf, for one thing. The doctor recommended I take it easy for a couple of days. I felt okay enough to play in the tournament, so I did; my leg was sore, but I don't think it affected how I played. Anyway, we lost, were eliminated, and headed home.

Prevent Injuries First

Injuries are a part of sports and I'm glad to say that since I've been playing, I have seen very few. Whatever mistakes adults might make in other parts of kids' sports, safety is not an area they would ever mess around with.

I've always felt the safety of the kids is more important than anything else, even more important than playing time.

The equipment, for example, is usually the best a team can find, from shin guards, to cups, face and mouth guards, to helmets. Before the season begins, parents should find out exactly what other safety equipment is required. As I discussed in Chapter 8, they should buy the best and make sure everything fits properly. It is impossible to be too careful or too cautious. Officials check the players to be sure the proper protective gear is being worn; in football, if the referees see a player not using protective gear, they can call a penalty.

All teams will have first aid kits handy, and many will have a least one trainer available at practices and games. To help prevent injuries, loosening-up exercises are now part of every team's routine before practices and games, and if they aren't, they should be. Pre-playing exercises are an important way for athletes of all ages to prepare their muscles for use. Although very young children might be pretty limber, it's still important for them to always stretch thoroughly before their practices or games. For one thing, it will get them in the habit of stretching so that as they get older it will become automatic. It's also a lot of fun, especially if the coaches get the kids laughing while they stretch. Parents will enjoy watching the kids do their warm-up routines, it can be very entertaining. Make sure the coaches allow enough time for the kids to loosen up properly. If they should start to skip or cut back on warm-up time, it's a good idea to remind them how important it is.

Another concern for young athletes is the risk of overuse. As a baseball pitcher, for instance, I am very aware of the dangers involved in too much pitching. I believe all children who want to pitch should have the benefit of a pitching coach at some point, either as part of a group or privately. Knowing the child and their arm, the coach will be the best judge of how many pitches the child can throw. In the early years, kids will play baseball on a small diamond. The distance from the mound to home plate will get longer each year. At ages twelve or thirteen, kids graduate to the full major-league distance of sixty-feet six inches. Some adjust with no problem; others may be straining to make strong pitches as the distance increases. A pitching coach will be able to recommend exercises to help make the child's arm stronger. I don't mean to criticize team coaches, but it's rare to find one with a good knowledge of pitching. Many of them think they know more than they do, and this can be risky. (Actually, pitching is one of those things a lot of people think they know a lot about.) My advice is to pick a pitching coach you trust and stick with him. Know how many pitches your child should throw in a game and stick to that number, too. Even if the kid is pitching great and the coach wants them to keep throwing, don't give in: when they reach their pitch limit, take them out. The child's arm is at risk and you shouldn't take chances — an overused pitching arm might not show symptoms or become a problem until the late teenage years or early twenties.

Coaching Tip for Coaches #3:
Give a Team Speech about Getting Hurt

From the very beginning, coaches need to give the kids some ground rules. Before the first practice, I think would be a good thing for every coach to make a speech to the team about getting hurt or sick. Young kids will only remember part of what the coach says and the topic of being hurt or sick needs to be emphasized, so make it a special, separate speech. (In fact, I believe this approach is a good one for coaches to use whenever they really want the kids to understand and remember what they're saying.)

First, the coach should make it clear to the kids that they must come out of the game and tell the coach immediately if they get hurt, or if they are feeling sick, even if it's only slightly. Coaches just can't see everything; with so many demands on their attention, they'll miss things that happen on the field, including injuries. So kids may have to take themselves out of the game if they're not feeling just right. Finally, the coach should let the kids know that if they fail to come out of a game when they should, they'll put them on the bench for a long while, no matter how good a player they are. And if they lie—about anything, but especially being sick or hurt—they will sit on the bench and not play.

Admit to Your Injuries

I have been guilty of lying about an injury. At an indoor baseball practice, I was wearing my spikes on my way to the pitching mound and I slipped and fell on a tile floor. I went right up in the air and came down on my right shoulder. It hurt some, not too bad, and since I'm left-handed I finished my workout. Unfortunately, after a few days the injury wasn't getting better, so I went to the trainer at my school, who said I needed to rest my right arm. When it still didn't get better, I went to my doctor, who said I needed to keep resting my right arm. But I thought it would be okay to at least go to practice, even if I couldn't do much. As soon as I walked in, my coach asked me how my shoulder was feeling and I said "Fine." It's not that I wanted to lie; I just didn't want to talk about the injury. I thought it was no big deal and that I'd be able to practice and still rest my arm. Still, no matter what I was thinking, I lied to my coach. The worst part was that my dad overheard me do it. Well, I can tell you, I got a pretty good talking to, if you know what I mean. It all worked out okay; my shoulder is fine and I learned another lesson. But I really did a lousy thing to my coach by lying to him. It kept him from knowing I was injured and not one-hundred percent able to participate; it could have hurt my team, too. I knew better and just plain said the wrong thing. As I've said, I am a work in progress, and I will do everything I can to not repeat a mistake like lying, to anyone, about anything.

If a kid lies about feeling sick or being hurt, it can be really dangerous. Whatever is wrong could be more severe than they realize and could get worse if they keep playing. When it comes to their safety, coaches and parents aren't the only ones who have a responsibility to kids. The kids themselves need to take some responsibility for their own safety. And if a kid has been sick or hurt at home, the parents need to inform the coach. I believe all coaches will appreciate knowing what shape their kids are in and if they still put winning above a kid's health then you just may have learned something about the character of the coach.

THIRTEEN
Burned Out or Turned Off

My family tries to schedule our vacation for when
the baseball season ends (I mentioned how this works
in Chapter 1). Since my dad and I both love to fish, we
usually go someplace where there is good fishing. Last
summer, right after my last baseball game, we went to
a cabin in the mountains on a lake with lots of big fish.
We had a dock in front of the cabin with a great motor
boat and from the first afternoon we were there until
the morning we left, I fished. I was either on the dock
or we were out in the boat exploring the lake for hot
fishing spots. Some mornings, I would wake my dad at
four o'clock to get out and fish and then we would fish
some more late at night. As I think back and write about
it, it seems a little weird. I couldn't do enough fishing;
it was like I was possessed. Not only was I fishing like a
madman, I was buying fishing gear like a madman, too. I
had been saving my allowance money for quite a while, so
I had a few bucks to spend and I made sure I spent every
cent of it. The guys at the fishing tackle store in the little

town there all knew me by my first name. As soon as our car pulled into their parking lot, the salesmen would knock each other down for the chance to wait on me. They ignored my dad, but they loved me: they knew I would buy anything they said might catch fish. Some kids love candy stores, I love golf shops and fishing tackle shops. I'm even hooked on the catalogues. If I studied Latin and math the way I study Orvis Fishing Catalogues, I would probably be better off, but I just don't.

Anyway, some afternoons I would sit on the dock by myself and think and fish. I did a lot more fishing than thinking. I caught almost a hundred fish and I loved it, I was happy. Fortunately, I was taught to be a catch-and-release fisherman; otherwise, my mother would have had a kitchen full of dead fish because we couldn't possibly eat as many as I was catching.

Now I realize my mind and body were telling me something. At the time, I didn't think much about it, but during the season, our baseball team had played about sixty-five games and competed in four separate tournaments. I'd also played some competitive youth golf. So maybe this was my way of winding down after a long season. I didn't even take my baseball gear on vacation. There probably wasn't enough room anyway, with all the fishing equipment I had packed. All I knew at the time was I did not want to play or even think about baseball for a while.

I'm not sure if it would be considered a form of burnout or not, but by the time each season ends, I'm ready to do something besides play the sport I just finished. I want to be able to relax and mess around when I feel like it, with no schedule to keep.

The Fatigue Factor

Parents often diagnose their kids as suffering from burnout. Often, I think it might be the kid is just tired. People tend to think that when kids get tired all they need is a good night's sleep and they'll be good as new again. This may be true with some kids in some situations. Still, there are a lot of ways for kids to be tired.

Adults consider kids' sports to be just another way of playing around and in a way they are, but as I hope I've proven by now, there is more to playing kids sports than just running around on a field or a court. There's more pressure than parents might think and it can take a lot out of a child. In addition to the pressure to be on time for games and practices, there is school work to get done. Then there is the pressure to learn their sport and improve their skills. They see other kids getting to be better players and they might feel pressure to try to keep up with them. Then, even the nicest coaches will apply some pressure to play well and to win. When all or even some of these pressures land on a kid, especially over the length of an extended sports season, it can wear a kid down and tire them out.

Also, some kids just don't love sports. They might like them okay, but they don't love the sport they're playing the way other kids do. Add the pressures I've just mentioned to a screaming coach, screaming parents, and the difficulty of learning to do difficult things in a sport you're not crazy about. Naturally, these children will wonder whether they want to continue playing at all.

Parents and coaches need to be alert for certain warning signs. If coaches knew what to look for—and I'll suggest a good way of getting up to speed in a minute—they could watch for kids who seem to be losing interest in the sport or not playing as well as they did. Kids who used to be cheerful and alert might be generally less focused. Kids who were nice might all of a sudden become behavior problems. I have seen these things happen and when it gets to a certain point, the kid might want to get away from their sport for a few days, or even permanently. Instead of just ignoring the kid and letting it go, coaches might be able to help.

Parents should encourage their kids to talk about how they really feel about their sport or their team or the coach. Take the time to just listen, real close. The kid might talk about something bothering them that the parents knew nothing about. Usually, there will be a way to fix the problem if everybody knows what the problem is. The kids might not be burned out, they might just have turned off for the moment.

Coaching Tips for Coaches #4:
Go Back to School

At every level of competitive sports, the best coaches are the best teachers. At the beginning of each season, I believe it would be a good idea for every coach to take a half-hour or so and sit down with an experienced elementary or middle-school teacher, to learn from an expert how to set up a set of learning objectives and how to communicate achievement. The coach could show the teacher their list of team goals (which each coach should have handy); explain what they hope to accomplish with the kids; and ask for suggestions and tips on the best way to communicate with and teach the kids. The coach could also ask the teacher the best way to monitor children's behavior and progress. In turn, the teacher could tell the coach about certain warning signs that might indicate a child has some problems that need to be dealt with.

I can't emphasize strongly enough how important I think it is for coaches to know their kids better than just as players. They're little people with thoughts, feelings, dreams, and fears, and sometimes even little people have problems. Coaches are more influential in a kid's life than most coaches care to think about. They're adult figures with authority, which makes them important to kids. Most kids really care what the coach thinks of them, and although some coaches might disagree, usually kids try their best and do want to win and please their coach.

Recharging Your Batteries

I've been lucky. My parents and I work hard to try to find the teams best suited for me. When I'm playing it's important for me to enjoy myself and to be happy with what I'm doing, maybe not a hundred percent of the time, but overall. There will always be times when things get tough, but ending the season feeling I've enjoyed myself is important to me and to my family. I think this is one of the reasons I've never actually felt burned out.

Another thing I like to do is diversify. I love doing lots of different things and some of them I like doing alone. When I play golf with my dad, we get to be together, but we're each playing our own game and concentrating on our own shots. When we go fly fishing together, we're on different parts of the stream, so I get to be on my own. At our house, there's an area with a lot of small stones. Since I was about seven, I've always loved to go there by myself with a broom stick and hit stones off into the trees. I have imagined every possible game situation while I'm hitting those stones, from my team's league championship to the World Series. I also like to play solo against Tiger Woods on my XBOX , and I like to shoot my pellet gun alone. I'm not antisocial or anything; I love my family, and I like my teams, classmates, and friends. It's more that I recharge my batteries better when I'm messing around alone.

Sometimes I even like to be by myself doing something people might think is silly—like trying to write a book! But I'm happy, relaxed, and it works for me. I think the parents of young athletes should remember to at least offer them chances to do things completely away from their sport. Then when it's time for them to get back to their sport and their team, they'll feel renewed enough to enjoy playing again. And if they're enjoying themselves, they are less likely to quit playing because they're burned out or turned off.

FOURTEEN
Role Models:
Everywhere and Everyone

Derek Jeter, the captain and All-Star shortstop for the New York Yankees, has been a role model of mine for about ten years. I feel about Derek the way a lot of kids feel about their role models— if in reality he's a jerk, I'd rather not know it. But from everything I hear and read and from what people who know him say, Derek Jeter really is a good guy. He is unselfish and places the best interests of the New York Yankees first, on or off the field. Whether it's laying down a sacrifice bunt, diving for balls up the middle, or keeping himself in the best physical condition, he is willing to do whatever it takes to help the Yankees win (which might be why he owns four World Series rings). As far as his social life is concerned, it seems to be quite active! But even with the close scrutiny he lives with everywhere he goes, he stays above controversy. He has demonstrated the value of a positive, family-oriented lifestyle and stays close to his mom and dad. He is also among the most remarkable athletes of the last twenty-five years.

I have been in Derek Jeter's presence on two occasions. Once was at Camden Yards in Baltimore when the Yankees were in town to play the Orioles. At the time, he was in the worst slump of his career, batting about .165. The New York papers were saying he was trying hard and struggling to find a way out of his batting doldrums. Just before game time, he walked over to the stands, and stood at the rail along the third base line, and signed what must have been more than a hundred autographs. I stood nearby and watched while I waited my turn. Very patiently, he smiled at each kid and kept signing their baseballs, hats, programs, or whatever they handed him, as if he was batting .340 and had all the time in the world. Derek Jeter did this for the kids at Camden Yards while nearby, a whole bunch of Oriole "fans" screamed filthy obscenities at him. As I watched Derek sign autographs for those kids, I couldn't help but wonder if it was the kids' parents who were screaming those curses at him. When it was my turn, I handed him my baseball and he looked me right in the eye from about two feet away. I looked back at him and said, "Breathe deep; keep your head still, swing for contact, and you'll hit." Now, I don't want to say I'm responsible for getting him out of his slump or anything, but that night Derek was three for four and went on to hit well for the rest of the season.

My family and I like to go to a great restaurant where a lot of the Yankees eat when they're in town. We know the people who own the restaurant and they told us about one incident with Derek that I think is worth telling.

Derek came in for dinner with a lady friend and they sat at a quiet table for two. A strange man came in and walked right over to Derek. He started getting nasty and demanding that Derek talk to him. Derek ignored the guy for awhile, then asked him to please leave them alone. The guy got loud and crude, so the waiters took him outside. When the owner went over to apologize for what had happened, Derek just said not to worry about it—the guy had been stalking him everywhere he went for about five years! If you've ever stood near Derek Jeter, you know he is very big and very well built. He could easily have tossed the guy through a wall, but he didn't; he just went on eating his dinner. For my money, not a bad role model.

Sometimes, I've noticed, former ballplayers say outrageous things to get attention and keep their names in the paper or get a mention on ESPN. When they can no longer make the news as players, they still feel the need to find another way to get noticed. A few years ago, a retired pro basketball player told the media he wasn't a role model and didn't want to be a role model. Even though he has the right to say whatever he wants, this remark was silly, not very well thought out, and he should have known better. Unless, of course, he was really saying, Please, I want everybody to think of me as a role model!

For Better or Worse

Today, whether they like it or not, every pro athlete is a role model to some kid. It's not something athletes can choose to be or not to be, like joining the Moose or the Elks or deciding whether they're going to be Republicans or Democrats. Unfortunately, a lot of the pros choose to behave in ways that make them lousy role models; but even these ballplayers are role models for some poor kids.

In fact, even if they don't realize it, I believe every person is a role model to someone. Obvious role models for kids are parents, teachers, coaches, and usually these are great choices. I think all adults should be constantly aware that they may be role models to some child, even when they don't know the child feels this way. Adults come into contact with children on television, at school, in neighborhoods, and through sports. The way the adults behave can influence a child more than they know. It may be a good influence or a bad one, but it's powerful all the same.

One thing I have noticed— it's nearly impossible for parents to assign the role models. Children have a way of finding and adopting their own, and will defend them right to the end. It could be a mistake for parents who disapprove of their child's role model to tell the kid how much they hate so and so. It might only make the kid like and imitate the person more. Parents shouldn't worry too much, though. With most kids, role models seem to have a short life. They come and go, and some kids have a new one every week or so.

Even if there might not be much parents can do to control what role models their children adopt, they can still expose their kids to the role models they feel will provide positive influences. My mom and dad are devout Yankee fans, so naturally I see a lot of them on TV—which is how I grew up admiring Derek Jeter.

Choosing a Role Model

My own take on role models is that I don't think it's necessarily about copying the way they act or dress or what they do, as much as it's about seeing how their positive traits, their successes in life, may fit into what you want out of your life. As kids grow, their role models change. For a while, Barney was my role model; then it was the late Steve Irwin, the Crocodile Hunter. I talked and dressed like Steve for a long time. I think he was terrific, and I still enjoy his old shows and I respect how he loved his animals. I love animals, but not the way he did.

I've had pretty much the same role models for awhile now. Every now and then, I meet people I admire and respect for different reasons, and I find myself trying to learn from them. I try to hang with kids I like and respect, and I think we probably take things and learn stuff from each other. Naturally, my father is my top role model for too many reasons for me to mention, and, anyway, I wouldn't want to embarrass him. I don't know if I would actually call them role models or not, but I also like James Bond (Sean Connery, of course), because he's so cool, and I like the way he talks and the way he handles his enemies. And I like Cary Grant because, well, because he's Cary Grant.

Some terrific teachers have been positive influences on me; my fifth grade teacher was one of them. We were great friends the whole year and he really helped me begin to see the value of learning and doing well in school. Up until then, I would study enough to get by, but I never really thought much about actually learning the stuff. It never occurred to me that what I learned this year might be important to know next year; I figured when I was done for the year, I was done with it for good. This teacher taught me the difference between studying and learning. He's a great guy. Of course he's also a Yankee fan. What can I say?

Just because someone is your role model doesn't mean you like everything about them or believe they're perfect. For example, I am a great admirer of the late General George S. Patton, Jr. To me, he is a fascinating person, and I never get tired reading about him and his life. On the other hand, he had a very foul mouth and I don't go there. I was taught that cursing is for people who lack the appropriate words to get their point across. Maybe Old Blood and Guts cursed because he spent so much time around other soldiers. In spite of his cursing, I think he was among the best military leaders in history.

Duke basketball coach Mike Krzyzewski is another person I admire a lot. His approach to coaching and leading young men impresses me. He has proven you can coach as a gentleman, and still have a successful basketball program at the highest collegiate level, year after year. And he does it at one of the country's top academic institutions. Joe Paterno and Bobby Knight are not exactly my role models, but they are people I also admire and like to read about.

It would be impossible to talk about role models for kids in sports without mentioning Tiger Woods. To me, Tiger represents all that is positive about sports—young people, and sportsmanship. From the time he was little, he worked, practiced, and behaved like the champion he has become. My father often reminds me of the fact that Tiger spends more time on the practice tee and in the exercise room than other golfers. I think it is interesting how the media sometimes complains that Tiger is too courteous, generous, and fair, and not controversial enough. I'll take behavior like Tiger's for a role model anytime.

The people I admire, and who are, in a sense, my role models usually have a few things in common. First, they conduct themselves like ladies and gentlemen. Second, they live with a strong work ethic. Third, they are willing to stand by what they believe in.

The Role Model is You

Hopefully, over time, as kids choose their role models, they will learn something from each one of them, even if it's a lesson in how not to behave. Ultimately, though, parents are the built-in role models. In some cases, kids use their parents as examples of what they do not want to become; they may love their parents, but they don't want to grow up to be like them. On the other hand, they may want to be just like their mom or dad. Either way, it is critical for parents and all adults to realize that their behavior and attitudes affect children more than they know.

Kids might be inexperienced in life, but we're not stupid. We usually see and understand much more than adults give us credit for. So, if you're ever tempted to get out of line at some kids' game, remember, there are children around you. Kids follow Yogi Berra's saying, "You can observe a lot by watching."

FIFTEEN
Parents:
The Beginning and the End

I have played in front of crowds, in critical game situations, in front of major league players, been injured, booed, and played against highly skilled, nasty, aggressive kids. But nothing frightened me as much or made me as sad as one incident I witnessed between games at a doubleheader in my early years as a ballplayer.

It was an away game and the weather was fairly hot. In those days, on that team, the kids were allowed to be with their parents between games, so my parents and I headed back to our car to get a sandwich and a cold drink. As we were walking through the parking lot, we heard someone yelling and cursing. We looked in the direction of the noise and saw one of my teammates and his dad. They weren't far away, but we were in back of a row of cars, so they didn't know we were there. What we saw was awful. The dad was holding his son by the front of his baseball shirt, screaming curses, slapping the kid's face, hard, and yelling something about how he'd played. The scene probably didn't last very long, but it sure seemed like it did. I looked at my parents, and saw my dad looking upset and puzzled. When the dad finally stopped hitting his kid, he pushed him into their car and drove off. We went to our car and ate in silence.

The kid was a good ballplayer; he always hustled and I liked him. I thought he loved the sport and tried hard. Later on, I heard his father had done things like this before. We never did find out exactly what caused him to go off on the kid that day, and I guess it's between the two of them. When we talked about it later, my dad told us he felt bad and didn't know whether or not he should have stepped in and tried to get the father to calm down. He said it's a very difficult decision to make and I agree.

I felt sad whenever I thought about the little kid and his dad. Seeing them like that left a big impression on me, because I really felt sorry for the kid; and, I felt scared. I was scared, because all of a sudden, I'd begun to realize that kids' sports must be a lot more important than I'd ever imagined. At least they were to that father.

From what I've seen in my ten years playing kids' sports, mostly all of the parents are nice people and good parents. Most of the time, you can tell they really love their kids and want the best for them. I'm happy to say, the reason I still remember that awful scene is because it was the only one like it that I've ever actually witnessed.

The Most Passionate Fans

Now, I don't know what goes on when nobody's around; what I do know is that parents will do anything they can to help their kids. And when I say anything, I mean anything. I would never say I've seen it all, but I've seen a lot. For one thing, parents are probably the world's most passionate fans. When I play first base, I'm close to the sidelines where the parents sit, so I have a chance to see and hear how they behave.

Parents are obsessed and their behaviors are driven by one primary objective—playing time for their child. This is another reason I call my book, *Playing Time*. To some parents, it can be an addiction; they crave playing time, the more the better; their child can never get enough. If they believe their child is not getting enough playing time, they will do whatever they believe is necessary to get them more. And if, for any reason, you ever say or do anything that might reduce their child's playing time, watch out—you could be in for trouble. If, on the other hand, their child is getting a lot of playing time, they will do whatever it takes to ensure their child continues to play a lot. (So be careful you don't get caught in the middle!)

If you attend a lot of kid's games, you will hear all kinds of things said—some good, some not so good. But one phrase you will probably never hear is, "Coach, my child has been playing a lot, take them out and give another kid some playing time." In fairness, there are certain situations where you just might hear this said.

Such as, if their child is being pummeled by another kid in football, or if their kid who's pitching has given up eleven runs in the first inning. Then and only then is there any chance you might hear this request.

I guess to help their kids to play better and play more, some parents believe in giving them coaching tips during the game. They must think their kid forgets everything about the sport the second they step across the white line onto the field. I have heard parents holler out the most complicated instructions you can imagine. If they yelled these things to Peyton Manning, I doubt he'd even know what they were talking about. Actually, at times, it can be funny. When I hear a parent yell something to a kid, I can see the kid look over with the most confused look, like they were just asked to solve an algebraic equation in their head. Every once in awhile, a parent will throw in a few curse words; I guess so the kid will pay more attention to the instructions they're giving. Now, the youngster is not only confused by the technical advice they don't understand, they're also embarrassed by the bad language.

Unfortunately, parents don't only yell instructions. When I was nine or ten, I was playing on a football team, and we were terrible; we couldn't beat anybody. We had about thirty kids on the squad and twenty of them wanted to play quarterback. During one game, the parents of our third or fourth string quarterback decided it was time for their son to play. They started to scream stuff about how badly our quarterback was playing. No matter what that little guy did, they screamed criticism about him, using his name. Just so everyone—especially the coaches—would pay attention to their directions, they started screaming curses at the kid as well. Naturally, the quarterback's parents weren't too supportive of this approach, so tempers and voices started rising. After what I thought was too long, our coaches finally had the parents evicted from the stands, and later banned them from both our practices and games. The quarterback felt lousy and so did the child of the screaming parents. It was a shame for everyone involved.

Parents in Perspective

The devotion parents have for their kids and their sport is amazing. I have been on some teams with parents who would never attend a parent teacher conference or a PTA meeting, but they would never miss a practice, let alone a game. At a lot of practices, you will see parents standing around in a group, each one watching every little move their kid makes. Our family calls it "starin' 'n comparin'." I guess as long as the kid doesn't care, it's great. I prefer having my parents drop me off for practice. They come back about fifteen minutes before it ends; they don't go far and with cell phones I can always reach them if necessary. This is our way but I know it's not for everyone. And with really little kids, I think the parents should stay close by. For one thing, the kid might get injured and need a parent to be there. Some parents depend on other parents to watch out for their kids. With little kids, however, I also think it's best if the parents watch their own kids.

I've noticed another group of parents. This one is not necessarily thrilled that their kid is playing sports. They might resent the time, the cost, or the inconvenience involved. Or, because the parents themselves have never played sports, they don't care about sports and don't even understand the sport their kid is playing. I feel kind of sorry for these families. It's a shame to see some kid make a terrific play and the parents don't even understand what happened. I've had some of these parents ask me the most basic questions about a game, things you would expect everybody to know.

I am familiar with this subject because my own mother was in this group once. When I first started sports, I don't think she really knew one sport from another. She would come along to the field to be sociable, but she never knew what was happening. She just watched the other parents—if they clapped and cheered, so did she. If they looked and acted unhappy with something, then she would, too. If my dad and I said the Yankees were on TV, she thought it would be a show about the Civil War. But I've got to say, she has sure changed. Now, she will discuss free agency, ERAs, who might be traded to whom, and the seeding of the NCAA Basketball Tournament, too. What a transformation! What a girl!

If a child really wants to play sports, I think the parents should at least learn the fundamentals of the sport, if only to show an interest and support their kid. If someday some major university offers their child tuition, room, and board, they might be glad they paid a little attention to their kid's athletics.

Speaking of college, another group of parents is very glad their kid is playing sports, but for another reason. They fully expect their children will grow up to be professional athletes. I don't mean they hope their kid will be a pro; they expect it. At the very least, they expect an athletic scholarship to a college. Now, parents usually think their children are much better athletes than they really are. As long as this kind of thinking doesn't hurt the kid or cause problems, I think for families to have dreams like this is a good thing. I use the word dreams, because that is what they are. There's nothing wrong with having dreams. I have lots of them myself. However, it is important to keep in touch with reality.

According to a 1999 study by the National Center for Educational Statistics, only one percent of all the kids playing organized sports today will qualify for a college athletic scholarship. As for playing sports at the professional level, you can imagine how small the percentage becomes. The odds are heavily against child athletes growing up to be professionals, or even college players. Of course, if you look at it another way, you know that some kids will have to make it to the pros, and that some will play in college. In the years ahead, somebody is going to be playing in the World Cup, the World Series, and the Super Bowl. When people turn on their plasmas to watch the Rose Bowl, the College World Series, or the Final Four, the schools are going to have to make sure they field players for the viewers to watch: so, why not your child?

Parents with pro ball dreams for their kids often

feel they were never able to fulfill their own dreams of athletic success. At the same time, they can't believe how easy sports are for kids today. They're devoted to starting speeches with the words "In my day" or "When I was playing" or "At your age I could...." In their day, the kids played better, the coaches were tougher, the weather was worse; they used tree limbs for bats and rocks for bases; they couldn't drink water, and they walked everywhere they went.

It's always fun to hear this stuff, but some parents go too far. They really expect their child to be like them (or how they imagine they were) only better. They want their child to do and accomplish all the things they didn't. It's definitely understandable: I know parents always want their kids to do better than they did. Like so many other things in kids' sports, it's fine, as long as it's kept in proper perspective. Kids are little people who all play, run, throw, kick, shoot and hit differently. Parents shouldn't resent it if their kid doesn't measure up to some imaginary standard. They shouldn't be upset if the kid happens to like a sport other than the one they used to play. And they shouldn't be angry or resentful if their kid turns out to be a better player than they were. I don't know whether it's true or not—I have no way of checking—but my father is always telling me I'm way ahead of where he was at my age. I'm glad he tells me that instead of the other way around. To keep my spirits high when we're practicing these days, he has a special saying for me, a paraphrase from a song in Annie Get Your Gun: "Anything I can do you can do better—except being me!"

Parent Watching: A Fun Spectator Sport

In a way, I think parents help make kids' sports more interesting and even more entertaining. They can be fun to observe. Sometimes I feel like the ape at the zoo who watches the visitors in front of his cage. As each new season gets under way, I see the different personalities of the kids and the parents start to surface. It seems as though every team I ever played on had its share of parents who were real characters. Like bases, goals and balls, they come along with the sport.

I played with one kid whose father was nowhere to be found at the try-outs and practices. But once the season started, his dad was at the fence closest to wherever the kid was playing. Before the game started, the kid would go over to his father for a chat. When each inning would end, on his way in from the field, the kid would run over to his father for a chat. When he was batting, the kid would look at his father before and after each pitch, and when he finished batting he would go over to his father for a chat. I never got to know this kid well enough to ask him if their chats were his idea or his father's. The kid was pretty good; maybe I should have tried to listen in on some of their little chats.

Another type of parent I've observed in action is the "team gopher." This is often a mother and father team trying desperately to win the coveted MVP Award, Most Valuable Parent. They're the wonderful people who are keeping the team from falling apart. They will do it all.

They will get driving directions to away games and tell the players to go to bed early, do their homework, stay out of the sun, use sunscreen, drink water, and go to the toilet. When you travel to a tournament, they will tell you where to stay, where to eat, what to eat, and where to get a good car wash. You name it and they are always ready to do good things for you. At one tournament, I wanted to ask them to book me a tee time at a local country club, but my mom shot me down. I'd figured why not—it would probably make them happy and give them something to do. As I'm sure you can guess, they were doing all these good works so the coach would like them and give their kid more playing time. Unfortunately, their kid wasn't much of a player. They would have had to get our coach the general manager's job with the New York Yankees for him to give their kid more playing time and even that might not have worked. They're nice enough people; they just went a little overboard for their child. There's a lot of that in kids' sports.

I've discussed the importance of playing time in Chapter 5, here, and elsewhere, but I really can't emphasize it enough. I have reached the conclusion that everything parents do, directly or indirectly, is designed to get their kids more playing time. When I was really little, my dad coached my basketball team. Parents were always bugging him to give their kids more playing time. He'd try, but it was never enough to suit them. Some of the parents even brought stop watches to time exactly how much their kids played. Finally, when they were getting on him at a meeting, he said he knew a good way for their kids to get more playing time. They were thrilled and couldn't wait to hear what it was. He just told them, "If you want to get your kids more playing time, go to a court with them and practice and give them more playing time—with you!" That year, the team parents did not vote my father their Coach of the Year. He just missed it by eleven votes out of twelve. I think my mom voted for him, but I'm not sure.

I don't say this just because my dad was my coach, but I think parents should avoid criticizing coaches in front of their kids. Once this starts, it is hard to control. Kids who hear their parents say negative things about the coach are likely to pick up on the gripe and use it as an excuse for their own shortcomings, or even contaminate the team by telling the other players their parents think the coach is lousy. If a parent has a complaint about the coach, they should go to the coach in private and talk it out. Teams don't need any additional friction.

Yet another tactic used to ensure playing time is for a parent to become one of the coaches. I've really seen this taken to extremes. One baseball team had seven coaches, all fathers of course. If you do the math, you can see how this made for a difficult situation. It's only natural that coaches will favor their own children and those seven kids were usually the starters, leaving two positions open for five kids to fight over. The team said how great it was to have so many coaches to teach the kids; but of that staff, only one or two knew much baseball and ever did any actual coaching. With an arrangement like this, the coaches become a little club that's very difficult to join. It may be wise to check with a team in advance so you know how many coaches they have; it might avoid problems later on. In baseball and basketball, for example, I have yet to see the need for more than three or four coaches per team.

Unlike the overly involved parents, another group just goes along and seems to accept everything. No matter what anyone does, it's fine with them. This may sound okay. In reality, they may do as much harm as any of the other groups. If the coach decides, at the last minute, to go to an out of town tournament, even if they're unhappy they won't object. I once played for a coach who cursed constantly, yet to the best of my knowledge no one said a word to him about his habit, not even my own parents. As a family, we didn't like it, but we figured the good outweighed the bad. I liked the team, the other kids and I were having a good year, so we went with the flow. Looking back, I think we should have told the coach how we felt. I believe we had that right.

Unless parents are willing to speak up properly, the coach's authority might get out of control. Many times, parents keep quiet because they don't want to upset or anger the coach. They might be afraid the coach will take it out on their kid by reducing playing time, so they just go along and take whatever comes. It can be a tough decision, but in the case of a surprise tournament, for example, I think parents who are going to be inconvenienced or who cannot afford to go away should confront the coach. It may turn out other parents feel the same way and they will be glad someone spoke up. Kids need to be able to trust that their parents have things under control and are looking out for them.

Performance-Enhancing-Parents?

Parents may not realize the impact they have on their kid's performance, playing time, and general enjoyment of the sport. Parents can embarrass their kids, never meaning to and never understanding the significance. When parents embarrass a kid, the kid wants to hide. When a kid wants to hide, he doesn't play well. When a kid doesn't play well, he is not having fun and he may start to want to quit the sport.

Following are a few descriptions of parents who I believe affected the way their sons played baseball. I will use the context of an at-bat to make the point. When a player enters the batter's box, all eyes are on him and on his parents! Every kid is aware of this.

Scenario 1

The ump calls the batter out – looking. The batter (and obviously the parent) thought the pitch was a ball. The ump thought it was a strike. Strike Three! Batter is out. Game over. The parent starts verbally attacking the ump. The ump says, "Leave me the F...alone." Inappropriate? Sure. However, Mom starts running around and shouting what the ump said ... and now she has shouted the F word at least six more times. If it was inappropriate for young ears the first time it was said, isn't it inappropriate the next half dozen times? Mature? Not!

Scenario 2

Dad doesn't like the way the ump called the game. He runs over to the snack stand and pleads his case to the concession stand workers. Confused, they ask, "Do you want any drinks or anything?" Smooth? Not!

Scenario 3

Mom must think she is dressing for the cover of Sports Illustrated Swim Suit Edition. Motherly? Not!

Scenario 4

Dad has a new girlfriend. The happy couple is experiencing a "movie kiss" in the parking lot. Thrilling? Not!

Scenario 5

Mom walking aimlessly around the sidelines, talking loudly, but no one is listening, about how her son needs to play more. Got playing time? Not!

Scenario 6

On tournament, Dad shouting while his son is in the batter's box, "We didn't pay $2000 to see you play lousy!" Smart? Not!

Scenario 7

For all the world to see, father and son fighting - physically and verbally. Gamers? Not!

In order for a hitter to hit well, he has to get comfortable in the batter's box – or at least try to. If he is uncomfortable, he will try to get the at-bat over with quickly. In addition, he leaves himself open for the pitcher to take the advantage. Kids who want to hide will not hit well. In one of scenarios I described, the boy hit clean-up the previous year, when I asked one of his teammates how he was doing this year, I learned, he was 0 for 54. Embarrassing a kid will bring a budding sports career to a screeching halt faster than anything else. Parents can apply this insight to any sport and any set of skills.

A Kid's-Eye View

Sooner or later, how a child really plays will be discovered and there is nothing any parent can do to change this. Kids will either grow to love a sport, commit to it and make the sacrifices, or they won't. I believe it must come from within the child and cannot be done for them or to them, not even by loving parents. I believe all kids should be given exposure to sports at an early age and should have every opportunity to play and improve as long as they want to and as long as it's fun. If the time should come when the child starts to lose interest in sports, if it becomes work and they're not having a good time, it may be time to look for other activities. It's not always the kid's fault and it's not always the parent's fault; maybe it just happens.

A *Time* article of July 12, 1999, reported that 73% of the kids who play organized sports will quit playing by age thirteen. I think this is terrible and I think it really needs to be investigated. When you look at this statistic, there's a lot to consider. These kids didn't all decide to quit organized sports when they woke up on the morning of their thirteenth birthday. Quitting sports is a process and must have been on their minds for some time. Some of them may have wanted to quit playing when they were eleven or twelve or earlier. Parents must keep an eye out for any signs that the child doesn't actually want to play. Try to see if they're going through the motions to please other people, namely their parents. If a child decides to quit playing, parents need to listen to the child, find out what they're saying, and find the real reasons. It might be a simple issue that can be easily fixed. Or, it might be the child doesn't like the contact, the coach, the hard work or competing. It could be any number of reasons. The important thing is for the parents to try understand the child's point of view. If the child is willing, the parents might want to offer them a chance to try other sports. Some kids might enjoy individual sports instead of team sports. Golf, swimming, gymnastics, and tennis are great sports for kids. I believe there is a sport for every child if they will just give sports a chance.

There are lots of reasons for kids to stop playing sports. One is having parents who put too much importance on playing sports. One is having parents who don't think playing sports is important. The way parents behave is another. I guess there's no way to prove it, but in my opinion, most of those 73% percent of kids who quit sports did it because of their parents. It would be funny, if some kids played sports because of parents and but most kids quit because of them.

I wish there was a way for all parents, just once, to get the chance to be a kid sitting on the bench during a game. I'd be willing to bet no parent would ever want to get out of line again. First of all, one loud annoying parent affects more than just their own kid; they affect the whole team, because everyone hears the person and knows who it is. Even when it's the parent of a kid you don't know well or don't particularly like, you feel embarrassed and sorry for the kid. Especially when the parents go after the umpire or the referee, the more they do it the worse they sound and the more it embarrasses their kid. Most of the time, kids will act like it doesn't bother them, but they feel it.

Just for fun, let's turn things around. Suppose one day a kid went to work with his or her parent, and decided to start yelling and criticizing everything going on there. The kid could walk into the boss's office and tell the boss their parent is easily the best (expletive) employee in the company. They could say they think their parent should have more responsibilities and get paid more money. Then they might tell the boss their parent should have a bigger office. They could tell the other employees the (expletive) boss doesn't know how to run a business. The kid could tell the boss they want to work there too, it would be better if they were nearby to coach their parent while they're working. Finally, the child might demand the boss do things their way, or the kid might take their parent and go to another company. By now, you get the picture. It might seem crazy, but is it really all that weird? If the kid insisted on going to work with their parent and acting like this every day, the parent might seriously consider quitting or changing jobs. Maybe they would have no choice.

As children grow older, parents can't always be responsible for how their kids behave. But parents are responsible for how they themselves behave. Many of the problems parents create could be avoided by using a little common sense and good taste. If parents would behave the way they want their children to behave, kids' sports might be a lot more fun for everyone.

For instance, my mom and dad happen to be non-drinkers. Not all, but most of the coaches I've played for were drinkers. As long as they're responsible, it doesn't make any difference to me. If the team goes for pizza and some of the coaches and parents have a few beers, that's their privilege. However, I've been to team cookouts where coaches and parents got really drunk and acted crazy in front of the kids. This is not responsible drinking: in the first place, it's a cookout for kids, not a bachelor party. Suppose the kids had decided to do a little pot and they all got high. How do you think the parents would feel? If there's a difference, I don't see it.

PLAYING TIME TIP
Something To Think About

Someone sent this to me in an e-mail—I don't know
where the story came from originally, but everyone
who knows kids' sports will recognize it:

A parent was making a breakfast of fried eggs for their
teenage son. Suddenly the boy bursts into the kitchen.

"Careful! CAREFUL! Put in some more butter!
Oh my goodness! You're cooking too many at once.
TOO MANY! Turn them! TURN THEM NOW! We
need more butter. Oh my! They're splattering, hurry
cover them. COVER THEM. COOOOVVEERRR
THEEEEMMM ALREADY!

"Careful! CAREFUL! I said be CAREFUL!

"You need to listen! Turn them! Hurry up! Are you
CRAZY? Have you LOST your mind? Don't forget to
salt them. You always forget to salt them.

"Use the salt. USE THE SALT! THE SALT!"

The parent stared at him. "What's wrong with you?
You think I don't know how to fry a couple of eggs?"

The son calmly replied, "So now you know what it
feels like when I'm trying to play baseball."

Hell or Heaven?

There's no question, being the parent of a kid playing organized sports is a tough thing to be good at. If parents push the child too hard, that's wrong. If they don't push the child hard enough, they're wrong. If they get too involved, it can be wrong; if they don't get involved, they're wrong. Meanwhile, parents work hard. When they come home, if they have a kid playing sports, instead of relaxing in front of the TV they'll have to take the kid to a game or a practice. If there's nothing scheduled, they might need to take the kid to a field or a court to practice with them alone. Parents always need to have the money ready to pay team costs and buy equipment. When vacation time comes around, instead of sitting on a beach with a book or playing golf or fishing, they might be attending a tournament. There, they sit on a wooden grandstand in 98 degree weather at a dusty field in the middle of nowhere. When the game is over, they'll stop for a quick burger and fries and head back to a motel, which has doubled or tripled its regular rate in honor of the out of town families attending the tournament. Instead of a shower, TV and bed, they now get to take the dirty uniform back to the car and try to find a do-it-yourself laundry so their kid will look sharp the next day—then they get to do it all over again. This might go on for six or seven days.

But wait, there's more. In a perfect world, the kid will play all the time and play great and be happy. But, in all likelihood, this will not happen every day or even much. Some days, since the coach is trying to be fair to everyone on the team, the kid will ride the bench, which will allow parent and child to both sit on a hard piece of wood for a few hours in the same 98 degree heat. (Maybe you could call it a bonding experience.) On other days, the kid might play poorly and be in a rotten mood, ready to bite the head off anyone who gets near them, especially a parent. That situation always makes for a lovely evening back at the old motel. All of this might sound like a lousy way to exist, but remember, millions and millions of people are all doing the same thing.

Why? Because some day, in some game, at some tournament, the little tyke at the center of it all might just kick the winning goal, score the winning basket, or hit their very first home run. Then, if you can ever stop crying and if you don't injure the child with your hugs, you will head home knowing it was the best six days of your life.

Just don't forget the main rule for kids who play sports and their families. No matter what happens, whether they win or lose, play great or play lousy: ALWAYS, ALWAYS, ALWAYS GO FOR ICE CREAM!

AFTERWORD

Reading *Playing Time*'s page proofs again before printing, it is noteworthy how some things change and some things remain the same.

Bobby Knight isn't coaching, Joe Torre is no longer with the Yankees, and while Tiger Woods is still a great golfer, we see that athletes may be great, but not perfect.

In light of this, the truth of Rudyard Kipling's *If* only expands: "If you can meet with Triumph and Disaster and treat those two imposters just the same..."

Those who play must be humbled and reminded that the worlds of sports and life really do share a similar playing field; each is built on aspirations, talent, hard work, rules, discipline, ethics, and just plain good judgment.

Tiger, who is a role model whether he wants to be or not, teaches everyone associated with sports, especially youth sports, that greatness without character is an imposter.

ABOUT THE AUTHOR

Quinn Cotter was fifteen years old at the time he wrote the first full draft of the manuscript for *Playing Time*. Now seventeen, he is still a student athlete living and playing in Baltimore, Maryland. Quinn has played competitive youth baseball, football, basketball, golf, and skeet shooting.

Filled with more experiences from high school athletics, plus new insights from having "been seen" by college baseball programs, Quinn's next book project will focus on student athletes who decide "to play longer." He is already making notes for the sequel to *Playing Time*.

Recently selected as a Pinkard Scholar, Quinn has been studying at St. Mary's Seminary & University and just completed his first college-level course, "Christian Foundations for Dialogue." Quinn is now searching for that special college program that will afford him an excellent pre-law education and allow him to play exciting baseball.

Quinn continues to dream of pitching for the New York Yankees, then becoming a lawyer.

ACKNOWLEDGMENTS

I want to thank my Mom for giving me the tools for success; in this case it was the shoebox and note cards that started this project when I was eleven years old. Thanks for this, and everything else, too. I love you!

I want to thank my Dad who would patiently listen to my sports stories and who said, "Quinn, you ought to write a book." My Dad is his own man and he has encouraged me to be the same. His guidance gave me the courage to say what I thought needed to be said and would be helpful to others on the subject of youth sports.

I want to thank Holly, my Golden Retriever, a playmate recently lost, who was the best outfielder I knew although I may not have known it at the time.

Liz Mackie, my editor, who dotted the Is and crossed the Ts while keeping my voice strong and clear. Thank you Ms. Mackie. Any chance you could edit my schoolwork? How about the SAT?

Laura Strachan, my agent, who believed I had a "compelling story, well told" when I was only fourteen years old and who passionately knocked on the doors of publishing houses until one welcomed me. Thank you very much Mrs. Strachan.

A big "thank you" to Barbara Meighan for her contribution to the book. Ms. Meighan "gets it." She always has. She has validated and supported my efforts in writing this book from its earliest format.

What an amazing feeling to have the greatest pitcher of all time, Jim Palmer, #22, contribute to *Playing Time*. As I look back on the process of writing and promoting the book, Mr. Palmer's encouragement will always be among the experiences I will treasure the most.

Mary Ann and Mimmo Cricchio, for introducing me to Jim Palmer, and for an evening I will always cherish spent with Mr. Palmer at their restaurant, Da Mimmo in Little Italy, Baltimore.

Thank you to former Gilman School Coach Marty Meloy, the quintessential baseball man in Baltimore, and my advisor and friend. While I'll miss seeing Coach sitting on the sideline, he will never leave the Greyhounds. Thanks Coach!

Thank you so much to Gregg Wilhelm and Kevin Atticks at Loyola University's Apprentice House. They also "got it" and gave *Playing Time* the chance to be heard so that kids across the country can play better, play longer, and smile more.

Thank you to the Apprentice House Student Project Team at Loyola—Greyhounds, too—for a lot of creativity, energy, and a willingness to listen to a kid, again and again.

The future of publishing...today!

Apprentice House is the country's only campus-based, student-staffed book publishing company. Directed by professors and industry professionals, it is a nonprofit activity of the Communication Department at Loyola University in Maryland.

Using state-of-the-art technology and an experiential learning model of education, Apprentice House publishes books in untraditional ways. This dual responsibility as publishers and educators creates an unprecedented collaborative environment among faculty and students, while teaching tomorrow's editors, designers, and marketers.

Outside of class, progress on book projects is carried forth by the AH Book Publishing Club, a co-curricular campus organization supported by Loyola University's Office of Student Activities.

Student Project Team for *Playing Time*:
    Elizabeth Nirenberg, '12
    Eryn Crane, '10
    Lauren Kimmich, '09
    Nicholas Marx, '09

To learn more about Apprentice House books or to obtain submission guidelines, please visit www.ApprenticeHouse.com.

Apprentice House
c/o Communication Department
Loyola University Maryland
4501 N. Charles Street
Baltimore, MD 21210
Ph: 410-617-5265
info@apprenticehouse.com

LaVergne, TN USA
02 June 2010
184757LV00006B/31/P

9 781934 074411